Published by
Carraig Mór House
Maudlintown, Wexford

ISBN
0-9544370-0-4

Design and origination by Chameleon Creatives

THIS BOOK IS DEDICATED TO THOSE MANY

SPORTSMEN AND WOMEN WHO HAVE LEFT THE

LEGACY OF THE BOAT CLUB

FOREWORD

It is said that competitive success is always important in sport.

Indeed, Wexford Harbour Boat and Tennis Club is extremely proud of the long history of its members' achievements, at both junior and senior level. However, I would contend that it is the volunteer ethic of our club - the "Yes, I will give a hand" - which is the essence of our spirit, our heart and our longevity.

Without doubt, the August Weekend Tennis Open tournament, the largest Open in the country outside Dublin, would not be the success it is without it. Similarly, it is this dedication and willingness to help, on the balcony and in rescue boats every Sunday during the winter, which allows us to run one of the biggest dinghy fleets.

Overlooking the beautiful river Slaney, Wexford Harbour Boat and Tennis Club has a friendly, sociable atmosphere for all, excellent facilities, and thriving membership. Both sports are strong within the club and there are ambitious plans for the future.

Naturally this has not always been the case. As well as the 'ups', there have inevitably been a few 'downs', and many are included within the chapters of this fine account of one hundred and thirty years of the club.

On behalf of all the members, I thank Eithne Scallan for compiling the illustrated club history so successfully.

Austin Pender
Commodore
Wexford Harbour Boat and Tennis Club

Impression of Wexford Dockyard circa 1904

CONTENTS

INTRODUCTION *1*

BACKGROUND *3*

BRIDGES *8*

THE BEGINNING *10*

ROWING *12*

REGATTAS *20*

WATER SPORTS *25*

TENNIS *26*

Illustrated Account of The Boat Club *34*

SAILING *46*

MOTOR BOATS *58*

THE PREMISES *60*

CHANGING ATTITUDES AND THE SOCIAL SCENE *70*

TUITION *77*

TROPHIES AND SPECIAL PEOPLE *79*

RESCUE IN ALL FORMS *82*

THE TWENTY-FIRST CENTURY *84*

ACKNOWLEDGEMENTS *86*

INTRODUCTION

MANY PEOPLE HAVE HELPED WITH compiling the story of Wexford Harbour Boat and Tennis Club; all had happy memories of the enjoyment found in the club activities on land and on water - almost all of them punctuated their account with 'there were always terrible arguments and rows in the club'!

It seems appropriate to mention this aspect of the club's history because the "rows" were part of its life; the rows sprang from social change, financial difficulties, different interests, and different priorities. They emerge from the earliest Minutes, from accounts of alteration of premises, proposals to move and decisions to change the name of the club.

The name of the club had a significance which might not immediately meet the eye. It started as a Rowing Club which explains the description Boat Club. Very soon afterwards - (more than one hundred and twenty years ago) tennis was introduced. Sailing in Wexford Harbour flourished even before the club was established. The title of Boat Club however, meant that in later years when both tennis and sailing became more competitive elements, neither group of participants felt that the name of their club was acceptable in entering for competition. It was apparently for this reason that The Wexford Sailing Club was established within the club, and in due course, the word Tennis was incorporated.

Other activities within the club included table tennis and darts, swimming, golf on The Lawn outside the pavilion, and then motor cruising, power boats, speed boats, water skiing and windsurfing. (Drinking, dancing and poker are perhaps not classed as sports). By 1997 the club could proudly claim a new field of action when Inshore Rescue was established on an official level (subsequently under the RNLI banner).

Club records are incomplete, but many sources have been consulted in compiling one hundred and thirty years of this story. Any inaccuracies or omissions are deeply regretted and, if there should be such, hopefully any annoyance generated will be outweighed by the interest and pleasure of this record of one of Wexford's most important and best loved amenities. While the rows were mentioned frequently, it was equally common to hear the remark 'We had great fun'.

Lafayette

Sincerely yours
R. Lisle de Jr
Captain 1905

WHEN SAINT IBAR LANDED IN Wexford Harbour in the fifth century, he was probably not the first boatman to enjoy the amenities, but possibly the first with the preaching of Christianity on his mind.

According to maritime historian John de Courcy Ireland, it is certain that before this, people came to Wexford county across the sea. It is even possible, he says, that inhabitants from elsewhere in Ireland came to Wexford harbour along the coast in skin boats or dugout canoes. Some time after the visitors bringing Christianity, in about 850AD, the Norsemen, or Danes appeared in Wexford Harbour, arriving as Vikings to settle in this sea-base for wintering their long-ships.

By the tenth century, Scandinavian seafarers had noted the shelter offered by the lower reaches of the Slaney and took full advantage of the situation for their expeditions. Scholars have described how the Vikings got their longboats as far as Enniscorthy, pushing and pulling when necessary, since, difficult as this was, there was no alternative as there were no roads. From sixteenth century fishing boats to twentieth century sailing cargo ships and the first steamer in 1919, Wexford Harbour continued as a flourishing centre of boating activity. Cots and gabards (flat-bottomed cargo boats which carried a sail and were peculiar to the Wexford area) were built on the Slaney and on some other County Wexford rivers throughout the nineteenth century, and the traditional cot is still in use. John de Courcy Ireland describes this craft as 'the famous Wexford cot, one of the longest lived and most seaworthy of all the traditional craft of north-west Europe'.

Sketch of a Gabard from the river Slaney

It was only after some fourteen hundred years of such boating as was inspired by necessity, that the concept of boating for pleasure evolved to any significant extent in the area of Wexford Harbour. Much detail on various aspects of the life where the Slaney meets the sea is provided in the anthology of Wexford Slobs and Harbour, *High Skies - Low Lands* compiled in 1996 by Rowe and Wilson.

Included are comprehensive accounts of fishing, shooting, angling, engineering and wildlife. The relevant and more recent setting for this book on The Boat Club probably starts in the early eighteen hundreds.

In the period from 1835 to 1852 much valuable information on the eighteenth and nineteenth century houses and other landmarks along the River Slaney came from such chronicles as *A Topographical Dictionary of Ireland* written by Samuel Lewis in 1837, *A Scottish Whig in Ireland 1835-1838* (The Irish Journals of Robert Graham of Redgorton) and *The Diaries of Thomas Lacy* in 1852. All of them would appear to have been compiled after the writer had worked his way up and down the river by boat.

Specific accounts of boating for fun on the Slaney and in the harbour begin to appear by 1812. In that year, a piece appeared in *The Wexford Herald*, 3rd April 1812 "The Slaney Club in assorted boats had a pleasant outing. A shot was fired and they set out up river."

Many of the fine nineteenth century houses along the river banks have or had access to the river by steps, pathway, or jetty. One such residence was Ardcandrisk, where the owners, the Deane Morgan family, had a steamboat. Sadly she ended her days on the mud of the estuary.

The Deane Morgan steamboat

The Hon. Mrs. Deane Morgan was eldest daughter and heir of Hamilton Knox Grogan-Morgan of the Johnstown Castle family. She is pictured below.

Hon. Mrs Deane Morgan.

Henry Meadows (inset) with his steamboat

Another family representing the 'landed gentry' - the Meadows - had a larger and more striking steamboat which is shown above and belonged to Henry. The names Arthur and Henry recurred frequently in this family which is associated with many of County Wexford's substantial houses.

A number of Wexford's prominent business and professional men from such families as Pettigrew, Elgee and O'Connor, had yachts in which they sailed in the area of Wexford Harbour and the Slaney Estuary around the period when The Boat Club was established. A photograph from 1893 shows the famous Pettigrew craft, *Ta Ra Ra* with R.W. Elgee at the helm, J.B. Pettigrew, T. O'Connor, J. Elgee and M.J. O'Connor.

There is a long history of boat building in Wexford, documented in many books and journals, but a notable producer of pleasure craft in the nineteenth century was certainly The Wexford Dockyard Company.

In the late eighteen hundreds, the Wexford Dockyard Company, Launch and Yacht Builders, advertised the fact that 'Some of our launches may be seen running in Wexford......' and a detailed submission in *The Yachtsman* in April 1902 refers to both the *Avenelli* and the *Pearl*. Their contributor first refers to a voyage on the 12-tonner *Avenelli* from Wexford, 'a first class boat doing well now for her new owner in Southampton'.

The publication goes on to give an extract from *The Log of the Pearl of Wexford*. The 32-ton, 43-foot *Pearl* according to the anonymous writer, 'gave every satisfaction'.

The light-hearted log explains that the notes would have been more comprehensive, but for the fact that one of the crew, when jumping overboard for a swim one hot day *'between the Isle of Man and Kingstown brought the notes and a bucket of potatoes overboard with him. He says he dived 36 fathoms and saw the introductory page of my notes being perused by three savage lobsters from that part of the ocean...'*. The crew weighed anchor at Wexford in June 1901, met a storm, during which 'the craft behaved splendidly', called at Wicklow where unfortunately their captain who weighed sixteen stone, sat on the skylight and broke it, then journeyed on to Drogheda. There they stopped to have a look at the Boyne Valley where they were taken by a jarvey, and which they concluded was a very nice place for a picnic but a bad place for a battle. The voyage continued to Scotland and via the Isle of Man back by Kingstown (Dun Laoghaire) to Wexford after about two and a half weeks. The article concluded *'All through the boat behaved remarkably well... not a single hitch... accommodation is splendid... Your readers will be glad to know that the Dockyard Company in Wexford are now building three similar launches, and these will be seen also at Cork this summer.'*

There was other activity in the world of local boating. *The Wexford Independent* in 1898 had an item about the launch of a Wexford built fishing boat from Mr. Simon Lambert's ship building yard in William Street, origin also of *The Dolphin* and *The Swan*. *The Antelope* had a mention around the same time, but on this occasion because she was in collision (the Pilot's fault). In three editions that spring of 1898 pleasure boats of 25 ft. and 20 ft. were advertised for sale.

An aspect of the boating background in Wexford, although not directly connected with The Boat Club, is the activity which took place across the river at Ferrybank and was connected with the First World War. This was the U.S. Naval Air Station at Wexford, and its story was told by club member Jack Higginbotham in Club Newsletter No. 9. In 1918 the Station was started by the British Admiralty, but was then taken over by the U.S. Navy. Located on the property at Ely House, it was organised, built and equipped to fight and destroy the German submarines within the area of the Irish Sea. At the peak of construction activities, there were twenty officers and four hundred and six men. Soon after it was established, war ended, but in the period of its activities in 1918 before the armistice was signed, several submarines were attacked and destroyed, and the records indicate that 'the rigid patrol kept up by the sea planes was responsible for the cleaning out of the enemy submarines from these waters'. The 'Yankee Slip' is still in place near Ely Hospital and the Riverbank House Hotel.

Hurricane Debbie

THE AREA OF PRINCIPAL ACTIVITY around the Club itself is bounded by the bridges which cross the river and estuary. It is therefore appropriate, as part of the background, to make brief reference to the history of these bridges. The first bridge - on the site of the present Wexford Bridge - was built in 1795, as was the first of the bridges at 'the Ferry of Carrig'. Both were designed by American Lemuel Cox, both were Toll Bridges, and both were proclaimed free (of tolls) in 1851. At Ferrycarrig the bridge was replaced in 1912, and again in 1980 and a detailed article by John Foley and Avril Harvey appears in *Crossabeg - the Parish and its People.*

Downriver a replacement bridge was found to be necessary by 1858 and an article by David Rowe in *High Skies - Low Lands* states that "the Admiralty ruled for a site about half a mile up river so as to allow more convenient shelter for shipping in the less exposed part of the estuary". Philip Pierce and Co., Ltd. obtained the contract for a wooden bridge just below The Boat Club, and this during its hundred years of existence was known as the 'new bridge'. It spanned the river from Crosstown to Redmond Road beside The Boat Club. (The by now 'old bridge' continued for some time as a footbridge into the town from Ferrybank). The 'new' wooden bridge by the 1930s was becoming dangerous and after some years of growing concern about safety, a

decision was made to replace the bridge with a new structure downriver towards the south, nearer the centre of the town at the former site, shipping requirements no longer being an issue. Meanwhile, tar barrels causing single line traffic to move from side to side became a familiar sight, and the upstream bridge was often referred to as the "barrely" bridge, pronounced Barley! Once it had been replaced it was eventually removed with some skill and good equipment by Peter Killian, and the pitch pine was used in various structures.

Taking the Eclipse from New Ross to Wexford to dismantle the old bridge were Dick Elgee and 1st mate Ollie Bent

The new bridge spanning the river from Ferrybank to the quay near Wexford's North Station, was opened in 1959. This one did not have a long life and the super-structure had to be replaced after only forty years. Replacement was carried out in a remarkable time of only ten weeks, traffic using Ferrycarrig Bridge in that period.

The latest 'new' bridge was installed on the same site using a counter-balance system and taking into account the height of the arches required for sailing boats. It was officially opened on a glorious day in November 1997.

Weather is often a factor which dictates the direction of the boat trip, and Derek Joyce remembers as a small boy going to The Boat Club with his father to go out sailing, and the boatman would always ask 'Mast up or down?' because the bridge was still in existence beside the club and it was important to know which direction the boat was to take.

Right - The old bridge and its derelict state
Below - The present Wexford & Ferrycarrig bridges

FOR DETAILS OF THE FOUNDING IN 1873 of Wexford Harbour Boat Club (as it was originally), the most popular source is one known familiarly as 'Bassett' the *Wexford County Guide and Directory* written by George Henry Bassett and published in 1885. It has been used as a source for Boat Club details in the *Journal of the Wexford Historical Society No. 9, High Skies - Low Lands* and elsewhere. (Long time club member Larry Duggan has a different version in that he maintains the club started off in 1872 by renting or buying land at the old North Station from the Railway Company).

However, the relevant chapter in Bassett's Directory is headed *WEXFORD HARBOUR BOAT CLUB, WEXFORD REGATTAS AND ATHLETIC SPORTS*. *'On the 14th May, 1873, the Wexford Harbour Boat Club was established at a meeting held in White's Hotel. Among those present were: Mr. Charles H. Peacocke, Mr. Ml.Devlin, Mr. James P. Devereux and Mr. Lawrence Devereux. Mr. Peacocke presided, and Mr. Devlin acted as secretary and treasurer. It was arranged that entrance fee should be one guinea, and that the annual subscription should be one guinea. After a couple of years the entrance fee was abolished. It was revived again in 1884, and fixed at half the original amount.*

A boat house was built at Ferrybank, across the Slaney from Wexford. The cost was £80. At the end of 1874 the house was blown away in a gale, and with it all the boats, with the exception of three or four valued at £20 or £30.

Boat Club training began in 1873. Thomas Pococke, of Putney, was employed; and again, in 1879, Robert Patrick, of Newcastle-upon-Tyne. Since then the Captain, Mr. M. A. Ennis, has saved the cost of a professional trainer, by doing the work himself; indeed, it is only fair to say that no trouble has been spared by Mr. Ennis in order to keep the club in as high a state of perfection as possible. The record which it has secured is exceedingly satisfactory. The first race for out-rigged fours at the Wexford Harbour Regatta in 1873 was won easily by Wexford against the Slaney Rowing Club of Enniscorthy. The Wexford Crew was composed as follows:- 1. G. M. Carroll, 2. N. Caulfield, 3. G. M. Power, 4. M. A. Ennis (stroke), John Perceval (cox)'.

In *The Wexford People* of that year, in May 1873, the items of interest to readers largely concerned Steamers, Harmoniums, Teas and Manures. (Much advertising space was taken by silversmith Thomas H. Richards, whose fine trophy donated in 1903 and topped with an oarsman, remains in the club's possession, although it is now a sailing trophy). There is in the paper however, a news item about Wexford Harbour Boat Club with details as given by Bassett. Concurrently there was a show running in Wexford's Theatre Royal (where Mrs. Deane Morgan of the steamboat mentioned previously, was a patron) described as a 'screaming farce' and called *Slasher and Crasher*. There is no indication of course that this had any connection with the new club.

Rowing was apparently very popular at the time and Carlow Rowing Club had a "Bivouac party" on the Barrow in June of 1873. Also around that time, alongside the news about Czar Nicholas visiting Pope Gregory XVl, there was other news in *The People* for boatmen: *'Rowing Notes. We gladly note that a convention among rowing men as to the Rule of the River is now almost un fait accompli. Henceforth boats meeting each other are to keep to the right. The want of some recognised rule has hitherto been a fertile source of annoyance - sometimes even danger - and the necessity for it has been daily becoming more urgent as the number of boats multiplied. The proposed arrangement deserves every support. It will alike improve coxwains' tempers and decrease fines for broken oars and damaged boats.'*

A later chapter in this book is devoted to Rowing. Other items as well were in the news of the waterways. It was in 1874, that a letter appeared in the *Wexford Independent* from *A Lover of Sport* which may have referred to a Regatta that year. The committee was praised but was being advised to think of 'placing a man at each turning post to report any fouling during rowing matches'.

The report in *Bassett's Directory* on the club's history continued: *'Early in 1875 a general meeting of the members was held. The Club was in debt £70, and matters looked the reverse of promising. Mr. M. A. Ennis was appointed*

Captain and Honourary Secretary, positions which he still holds. There also was an executive committee appointed, and an effort was promptly made to repair the losses of previous years, and get out of debt. A piece of land was secured from the Dublin, Wicklow and Wexford Railway Co., beside the bridge which crosses the Slaney, and a house, slip, and embankment were built and the grounds enclosed with an ornamental railing. New boats were purchased, and, in fact, nothing was left undone to put the club in a position second to none in Ireland. Since 1875 there has been an expenditure, with this view, of upwards of £1,000, and the debt has been wiped out. The club-house is very agreeably situated, and has, since 1883, added to its undoubted attractions that of a tennis court, 150 feet long, and 50 feet broad, the land for which was also obtained from the Railway Company. The first tennis tournament was held in 1884'.

In May 1973 the club celebrated the centenary of its foundation. Little has been found on record regarding that centenary occasion, although some members recall the celebratory party which ended with a sunrise swim at Curracloe. A note in *The People* newspaper that year in referring to the centenary, mentioned that 'the Wexford Harbour Boat Club with a terrific stretch of the River Slaney at its disposal, is one of the finest of its kind in Ireland, and, indeed, is the envy of many a visitor from near and far'. The reporter Eddie O'Keeffe commented further that 'the Harbour Boat Club's annual dance for the Lifeboat Institution is a formal dress affair and always a highly enjoyable function'.

WEXFORD HARBOUR BOAT CLUB.

THE WINNING CREW.

J. Huggard (cox)
M. Kavanagh (bow)

G. Ashmore (No. 2)

M. Kavanagh (Bow)
J. Huggard (cox)

P. C. O'Connor (stroke)

L. J. Barker (No. 3)

L. J. Barker (No. 3)

P. O'Connor (Stroke)

We have pleasure in presenting our readers with a picture of the Wexford Harbour Boat Club four who are rowing so splendidly and successfully this year, and who have been the first for a long time to bring back an aquatic victory to Wexford. Their cups include two won this season, the Liffey Cup won at the Dublin Metropolitan regatta, and the Pierce Cup regained by them in home waters last week. The wins were particularly popular, as three of the lads are out and out Wexford townsmen, born and bred, and Mr Ashmore, who comes not far from Newtownbarry, fully shares their popularity, being not only one of the best but one of the most genial oarsmen on the river. The week after next the Wexford Harbour Boat Club crew will compete at the Limerick Regatta, and in the same week also at New Ross and Waterford, thus concluding the season. We have high hopes of their success, and wish them an unbroken record of victory.

The photograph, which is a excellent one, is by a local artist, Mr Charles Vize, who has here given further evidence of his ability and finish in technique as an up-to-date photographer.

WHILE THERE WAS, IN AND BEFORE 1873, a considerable amount of sailing on the Slaney and in Wexford Harbour, it is clear that The Boat Club was initially a Rowing Club. The success of Fours, Eights and Scullers, as outlined in the Bassett's Directory article, indicate that Rowing flourished at Wexford. A newspaper account of 1886 gives a very flowery account of WEXFORD HARBOUR BOAT CLUB RACES, from the Aquatic Correspondent; *'Undeterred by the nasty southerly squalls, the torrents of rain, the thunder's roll and the lighting's flash, the "boys" of our Harbour Boat Club fearlessly donned their aquatic colours on last Thursday to compete in their annual races'*.

Names and results were given, and a comment that 'they were very good, even against fearful odds' and that 'the popular captain of the Club, M. A. Ennis, rowed 25 miles midst all the wind and rain'. There was a further remark that 'the attendance of spectators was small in consequence of the inclement weather, and of course only a few of 'the Belles of Wexford' dared to face the opposing elements'.

The remarkable oarsman M. A. Ennis won at the Kingstown Regatta in 1879 and his team won at Carlow and on the Slaney in 1880 as well as securing the Irish championship Eblana Cup at the Metropolitan Regatta in 1882. A photograph taken by the eminent Charles Vize shows the winning crew, sometime between 1895 and 1915.

Rowing continued to flourish well into the twentieth century. Before the first world war

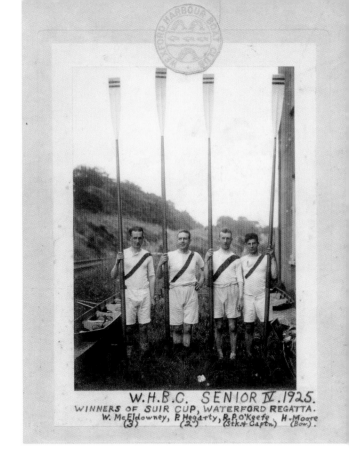

W.H.B.C. SENIOR IV. 1925.
WINNERS OF SUIR CUP, WATERFORD REGATTA.
W. McEldowney, P. Hegarty, R. P. O'Keefe, H. Moore
(3)   (2)   (Stk.+ Captn.)   (Bow).

the 'Oxford' boat was purchased and an extension of the storage area had to be built for the rowing Eights. Locally they were referred to as 'needle boats' and crowds would gather to watch them practising. The Railway had reached Wexford in 1872, and as the teams and their boats travelled to regattas elsewhere in Ireland, transport of the boats was by rail and taking advantage of the proximity of the club premises to the railway line, arrangements would be made to have the train and its wagons stop beside the club where the boats were loaded - and unloaded on return. Two wagons were required for the Eights (which perhaps did not divide in two at the time) and Eoin Murphy relates that the hire charge for a wagon taking a boat to Carlow was £4.10. The evocative photograph above of one of the Fours in 1925 illustrates the proximity of the railway line to the club.

In his recollections of the Wexford Harbour Boat Club, going back to about 1912 (although written in 1968), the late R. P. O'Keefe said: *'My brother rowed in Junior IV in 1913 and 1914. This Four was almost unbeaten, and won their events at Dublin Metropolitan Regatta, Cork, Waterford and Limerick Regattas. This Four was as follows; Timothy Keating (Stroke), Addison Hadden (No. 3), Willie O'Keefe (No. 2) Alphonsus Crean (Bow). All these gentlemen joined the British Army on the outbreak of the Great War in August 1914. They were all awarded Officers' Commission shortly afterwards. Tim Keating and Willie O'Keefe were killed in action in France in 1917. Addison Hadden was a prisoner of war in Germany for about a year before the war ended in 1918, and Alphonsus Crean died shortly after the war about 1921. The last surviving member of this crew, Addison Hadden, died a few years ago'.*

His notes on the family letterhead, include the remark 'Mr. W. J. O'Keefe, Faythe Maltings, Faythe House joined in about 1879'. Worthy of a visit is the O'Keefe commemorative stained glass window in the Church of the Assumption in Bride Street in Wexford, designed by Harry Clarke and erected in memory of the young Willie O'Keefe.

Raymond O'Keefe continued in his memoir *'I joined the Club in 1922. I had previously rowed for Dublin University (Trinity) in 1920 and 1921. There had been no competitive rowing between the years 1914 and 1921, when efforts were then made to revive it. I became Captain in 1925 and stroked the Senior IV, which was the first winning crew since 1914, when we won the Senior Challenge Cup at Waterford. I actually gave up rowing in 1926. The Garda then took on the rowing activities in the Club from about 1927 to 1931'.*

Details from the stained glass window in Bride Street Church

Exceptionally comprehensive material was made available to the writer by Michael Johnston, expert on the history of rowing and author of an outstanding book *The Big Pot*. In the late 1920s the rowing activities in Wexford were indeed taken over by the Garda Rowing Club as mentioned in recollections of many people and as supplemented by the detail from records of An Garda Siochána kindly provided by the helpful personnel at the Garda Archives. This valuable data from both sources has, of necessity, been condensed as this book is not intended as a record of results. Some of the details, however, help to paint the picture of boating activities of their period and the manner of reporting.

An item from *The Garda Review* of July 1928 is headed 'Foot-and-Mouth Disease v. Wexford Garda Sports'. The explanation is that *'the recent outbreak of foot-and-mouth disease called for all possible attention from the County Force, and therefore the time which should have gone to training for this big annual event had to be directed to the immediate suppression of the above epidemic'*.

Added to this was *'The Park, Wexford, where the recent Sports were held, being in extremely bad condition, and the amount necessary to put same in suitable order for Sports being prohibitive, even if time now permitted'*. All was not lost however. *'Notwithstanding the above disappointment, I am pleased to be in a position to state that the Wexford Gardaí are promoting Rowing in their Division, two teams, 'The Juniors' and 'The Maidens' (attached to the Wexford Harbour Rowing Club) are working strenuously to be in a position to compete at the Tailteann Games, 1928, at which they hope*

to share some of the laurels of Victory.' This report came from Sergt. A. J. Lee, 2185.

By August 1928, *The Garda Review* published another, somewhat dramatic, account of the Wexford Garda rowers. Under the heading REGATTA; *"The Wexford Harbour Boat Club has been further augmented by Gardaí from Divisional Headquarters. At the Waterford Regatta, held on 5/7/'28, both the Junior Fours and the Junior Eights were won by Wexford Harbour Rowing Club, and it is of interest to relate that there were actually seven members of An Garda represented in these races.*

On their return to the slip the Junior Fours had a most thrilling experience as a result of a motor launch having misjudged its distance and violently striking their (the Junior Fours) boat, rendering it unseaworthy - very much so too as it was "rammed" to such an extent that it split in two and disconnected itself from its occupants who were left to the mercy of the sad sea waves. Luckily, however, our brave oarsmen were not to be "let down", so to speak, and created a considerable amount of excitement and applause to the many thousand of spectators who cheered them as they gallantly came to shore in addition to showing the public in general that the Garda can do much more than row a boat. Casualties Nil!

But alas! The accident was to have its sequel, as the 'Maiden Fours' were to have competed in the boat which had been 'rammed' and not being 'Achievers of impossibilities,' their entry alternative was to "carry on" in another boat, which they did, and in consequence of this most unfair handicap - this unavoidable change - through lack of experience, of course, of this particular boat, the race was lost.

It is of interest to relate the preparations for Wexford Regatta are now well in hand for the carrying out of which many Garda from the country will participate.'

Later that year, in October 1928 *The Garda Review* published further news submitted by Garda Cornelius Driscoll and headed: *Tailteann Regatta, "Cork City"* in which he gave detailed results of winners. It concluded with the note that the 'serious handicap of inferior and obsolete boats' prevented them from winning their races, and how, 'but for the accident' (of the broken bow slide) 'the Wexford boys would have secured the laurels'.

In fact records show that An Garda Síochána at Wexford 'had for two seasons been chosen to represent the Wexford Harbour Boat Club and had won at every regatta outside of the Tailteann'. Reports for 1929 showed that 'Training is now in full swing'. In November of that year the Garda Review published a photograph of the Wexford Harbour Boat Club Senior Eight. (Not all were members of the Garda force and the photograph also appeared elsewhere).

WEXFORD HARBOUR BOAT CLUB
SENIOR EIGHT AND FOURS. 1929.

Back Row: T. E. Pierse (6), P. Sheils (5), C. Driscoll (7), J. A. Pierse (4).
Front Row: P. Wall, (Stk)., F. McCarthy (3), J. F. Kehoe (Cox), C. Sheridan (2), J. H. Moore (Bow)

The seemingly last entry regarding the Garda rowing activities was in *The Garda Review* of May 1930 with a brief note: 'Wexford Boat Club opened about 17th March and thirteen members of the Garda are now in training for rowing'. Recollections of members, and the club records, suggest that the rowing crews of the time, with garda members being the main crew, travelled to many regattas and got into financial difficulty - allegedly to the amount of £200. There is a suggestion that the end of the association lead to a certain amount of bitterness and a gap in activities. At a time when the club was again - or still - experiencing financial difficulties in 1933 the committee 'agreed to write to General O'Duffy pointing out the position of the club, and mentioning that this was brought about by the rowing activities of the Garda who had now all resigned!'. Raymie O'Keefe had a note in his memoir 'The rowing began to decline about that time, and an interest in sailing started about then'.

In contributing material, the authority Michael Johnston quotes such reliable sources as 'a very rare little book entitled *Dublin Metropolitan Regattas 1869 - 1892,* by RM Peters who was the Aquatic Correspondent of the *Irish Times*; and Forde Hall's *History of Boat Racing in Ireland*, published by the Irish Amateur Rowing Union in 1939'. He found Wexford Harbour Boat Club is listed in Peters as one of the clubs that had raced at Dublin Metropolitan Regatta by 1893. Their club colours are given as Crimson & White. The second source, Hall, notes the club as having been one of the members of the Irish Amateur Rowing Association in the early 1880s.

By 1935 the WHBC is not on the list of IARU Blue Book affiliated clubs.

Various records show that in the 1920s and 1930s the club seems to have been quite active and successful, WHBC teams winning in Waterford in 1925, Cork and Waterford in 1927, Waterford again in 1928, Galway, Limerick, Dublin Metropolitan and Waterford in 1930, and Galway once again in 1931.

In those days, Michael Johnston explains, "there were three grades of rowing: senior, junior and maiden, which nowadays would be called senior, intermediate and novice". From old programmes he provided details of the winning Wexford crew at Junior four in Cork in 1927 and at Metro, as well as runners up in Cork in 1930. The crew also won at Limerick. He felt that the quite high weights of the crewmen confirmed that they were probably mainly robust members of the Garda force. Michael Johnston found it interesting that the trainer was listed as E. Barry and he wondered if he was a member of the famous English family of watermen named Barry. Certainly Lew Barry was coaching professionally in Ireland at the time - at Galway - and much later the same coach was in charge of the Garda Siochána Boat Club, which he found an interesting link.

Club records in Committee Minutes over the years contain fairly frequent references to the rowing activities of the club. They noted that newspapers in 1931 had described the Wexford Harbour Senior Eight's win in Galway as 'The Sensation of the Day'. The Committee noted 'more good results' but there was a good deal of haggling over entry fee costs. In 1931 the cost of sending the boats by rail to Galway was £3.14.6. By 1933, when there had been no entry in the Minute Book for a year, it was noted that the club debt was now £128.9.6 and the Committee agreed to a proposal to wind up the club and to attempt to pay off some of the debts through the sale of the club cups and trophies which were to be valued. It was further agreed to consider an auction of the boats, and to write to all the clubs who might possibly purchase boats. (An offer from Carrick-on-Suir was subsequently up for discussion). There had been a special storage frame for the Garda boats, and they gave notice in February of 1931 of their intention to remove their boats. In a Minute of 1933 however, it was agreed to allow restricted use of outrigger boats and premises free of charge to allow the Garda to practise for the Garda week Regatta.

There is no precise written record concerning the decline of rowing as a competitive sport, and the club did not apparently wind up its existence. A number of Wexford people have their own recollections of rowing activities. Murth Joyce recalled that for himself and friends like Seán Scallan, rowing club boats up the Slaney and into the Sow River at Castlebridge was a favourite way of spending an afternoon, with a picnic in Eden Vale. Families living in their houses by the river would take out their small clinker-built sail boats for about a month in the summer, launching them with some ceremony. Eoin Murphy, former Honourary Secretary of the club, remembers that there were indeed financial problems in 1926 or 1927 and a

fund-raising auction when sculls went for 3/6d. There was some fiscal recovery after a few years, and skiffs were purchased from Nortons of Athlone (12 ft. long and 4 1/2 beam) complete with oars and rowlocks for around £7. Buying and selling of club boats was a recurring theme up to about 1937.

While club skiffs became more popular for casual rowing, the long outriggers continued in storage high up across the beams in the boathouse, no longer used and in a state of decrepitude. Kevin McCormack also referred in his memoir to the resting place of the boats, and the club pictures of rowing teams which included his father. *'In the early days it was all oars and blistered hands and action. There were six skiffs, built in Athlone, with wicker work seats and back rests and ropes back to the tiller. In addition, there was one general purpose punt, and all these were for the use of capable members. Ladies were not allowed to take out a skiff, unless accompanied by a capable male member.'*

George Bridges described the rowing of the Skiffs (which get frequent mention in the Minutes). He said they were built for one oarsman with one, two or even three passengers, and while there were occasional races, they were mainly pleasure boats. Members used club boats to row to such points as Artramont across the river upstream, and the caretaker was responsible for control. Nicky Furlong remembers them as 'miserable skiffs'.

In club Minutes for 1940, in preparation for Gala Day, there were further warnings about the boats which were 'for use of members only. Skiffs not to be used as tenders. Punt to

be used for that purpose only'. In the Minutes of June 1941 came the news that a punt had sold for £5 and another punt had been bought by Mr. Coffey for £8. In June 1947 the Committee was discussing boats again, and sale of the two outriggers was to be considered. Reference to movement of skiffs and punts was frequently in club Minutes. Movement could be an appropriate term, since periodically they seemed to go missing, or were reported as having been 'found' again. By 1949 things were beginning to liven up. Not alone was £6.10s to be spent on a raft, but purchase of two new sixteen foot skiffs was being considered. It was agreed to commission Mr. Ennis to build them for £20 - £25 each. (In the 1980s, club punts were being sold for £100).

It was seventy years after its foundation before there was any mention in the Boat Club records of members' own boats. At that time the committee went so far as to agree on hire of skiffs to visitors. A year later, in 1954, they were still discussing disposal of 'two racing boats', and replacing the old skiffs was also under discussion. In 1961 the committee was faced with the news that club boats had 'landed on the Ballast Bank', and agreed that there must be NO landing 'between the Bacon Factory and Ferrycarrig'.

There seems to be little rowing today. For a while there were canoes around the club. In 1989 there was an arrangement with Brother Smithy, canoe enthusiast and teacher, that he and his young canoeists could join the club. In 1990 there was a move when visitors came from another club for discussion, but Wexford members showed no interest. With the growth of 'coastal rowing' in the late 1990s, the Club occasionally made its facilities available to visiting teams although not themselves participating. To a limited extent, junior members row near the club, and compete when there is a Slaney Rally of the Inland Waterways branch. Sailors may be rowed out to their boats but there is no racing from the Club. According to the records, one venture into rowing of a different kind came about in 1988, when the club agreed to be involved in the project of rowing the Viking replica ship from Dublin to the Heritage Park in Wexford.

THE REGATTA AS A SOCIAL AND sporting event finds mention in newspapers and other records from quite an early date. Apparently Mr. William Coghlan, J.P. even before The Boat Club was established took a leading part in getting up aquatic sports. He started the annual regatta in 1838 and went on to help with the annual Rosslare regatta which was begun in 1883 at which time he said he had determined to leave to younger men the duty of managing future regattas at Wexford.

Still in 1873, that first year of the club's existence, a newspaper search - bypassing entries concerning Garibaldi, and Home Rule - reveals an item headed:
'WEXFORD HARBOUR REGATTA - We are glad to announce that a committee has been formed for conducting the annual Sports, which are to come off about the middle of next month. Programmes containing particulars will be published in due course. We trust the gentlemen who have kindly consented to carry out the Regatta will be generously supported by the public. William Coghlan Esq., Collector of Customs, acts as Treasurer and Mr. W. Caulfield, Esq., as Secretary.'

A detailed account of the Regatta appeared in *The Wexford Independent* issue of August 3, 1873, as well as *The People* of September 6, 1873, where it was described as *'one of the most successful aquatic fêtes which has been our good fortune to chronicle since the institution of this annual event upon the bosom of our spacious estuary... it is highly probable that but for the establishment of the Wexford Boat Club the revival of these sports could be indefinitely delayed... Some of the active spirits who promoted the sports on former occasions had been called to new spheres of duty...'.*

There followed details of organisers, those in attendance and the courses for racing events. Races for twelve classes were described: First Class Sailing Cots (the race admitted to be one of the best that has been seen in the harbour), Wherries with the exception of a Cutter, Four-oared Seine Cots (engaged in fishing that season), Second Class Pleasure Boats, Four-oared Ships' Boats belonging to the port not exceeding 18ft. in length to be pulled by sailors or men employed on the Quay, Four oared Pleasure Cots, Four-oared boats not exceeding 25 ft., First-class Outriggers to be pulled and steered by members of a recognised Rowing Club, Pair-oared in-rigged clench built to be pulled and steered by members of a recognised Rowing Club, Punts to be pulled by one man, Sculling Ships' Boats, Shooting Floats. According to the report, following the 'conclusion of the Aquatic sports' there was a display of fireworks.

Fireworks actually continued to be a feature for some time as a lady who remembers the 1920s and 1930s, Hazel Rowe Graham, has commented 'I remember a big regatta in about the 1920s with a wonderful fireworks display in the evening from the Ballast Bank; we went down to see it from the window of Thompson's on the Quay'.

The Wexford People, in September 1876 had a comment on the Wexford Harbour Regatta; 'but for the establishment of the Wexford Harbour Boat Club, we would have no regatta'. Success for the club's Senior Fours was reported from the Wexford Regatta of 1879, and then in an article on Social Life in 1885 by Fionnuala Nolan in the *Journal of the Wexford Historical Society No. 9*, the writer says Regattas were very colourful and entertaining affairs with bands playing. She quotes from Bassett "As well as providing an opportunity for boating and admiring nature, balls, dinners and meetings were regular occurrences. In 1885 the Wexford Boat Club presented their Captain, Mr. Ennis, with his portrait". Unfortunately, research has brought to light only a poor copy of a portrait of M.A. Ennis who does indeed deserve to have a commemorative photograph in this book,

as he contributed enormously to the early life of the club, as oar man, trainer, captain and organiser.

M. A. ENNIS

Newspapers in 1893 reported on the Annual Regatta of the Wexford Harbour Boat Club. The Band of the Third Royal Irish Regiment was present. There was a challenge match between the Cornwall and Wexford crews for the Seine Cot Championship of the Slaney for which £5 prize money was subscribed. Details follow, and also a report on the water polo match, and finally a note that a "duck hunt" concluded the programme. In March 1897 the Boat Club Chairman Mr. Peacocke expressed his regret that they 'had no crew on the river'. He said they had a splendid boat club, and they had money - and would get money, and they should be able to organise a crack crew. He could not understand why there was such apathy amongst the members on this important point. *The Wexford Independent* of July 1898 had reported some grumbling at the lapse of the regatta, saying there was no event of the year so popular amongst the people as the Regatta. A large meeting was held subsequently to promote the event and must have been successful.

By 1898 the Wexford Harbour Boat Club was mentioned again in a report on the AGM held at The Ballast Office. M. A. Ennis was reporting on behalf of the secretary and said he was in a position to state that 'your club house, boats and property generally are in a thoroughly efficient condition and your finances exceedingly prosperous'.

The Chairman C. H. Peacocke again expressed surprise at the apathy among members regarding having a crew on the river. Another three months went by before there was a report of election of a new Hon. Sec. in the person of Mr. John Elgee. The Elgees were a distinguished Wexford family, (associated with Oscar Wilde), and in three generations contributed significantly to The Boat Club. An early photograph shows Richard Waddy Elgee, Club Captain from 1905-1908 (see page 2). John Elgee was a prominent member and officer for many years, from 1898, and later another Richard (Dick) Elgee was well known as a sailor in the club.

In those years at the end of the nineteenth century, an unusual activity was reported from up the Slaney when at Scarawalsh a seven foot sturgeon was taken from the river.

A further somewhat surprising entry regarding another local sport was headed: 'WEXFORD ARCHERS. The Wexford Toxophilites held their annual meeting and agreed to add the game of croquet to the outdoor amusements of the club, in addition to their shooting meetings'. Among the other sports mentioned at that time was cycling. The Wexford Independent Cycle Club was established. There had already been successful athletic sports in Wexford in September 1884 'participated in by the Wexford Bicycle Club, which Mr. William Timpson has done so much to keep in a respectable state of efficiency'.

Evidence of the public's support for the Regatta around that time may be seen in remarkable photographs from the period preserved on glass slides in the deVál collection.

Regattas continued to be a successful event into the twentieth century, whether at the Quay in the town or around The Boat Club premises. References to Garda participation are included in the Rowing chapter. In 1919, there was a mention of the "very boisterous" weather for Ferrycarrig Regatta, and also, in August of that year, 'The Regatta - under the auspices of the Wexford Harbour Boat Club - a regatta under IARU Rules will be held on Thursday next, embracing 12 events including two challenge cups, Richards cup and Pierce & Co. cup. There is also a ladies' race'. A further report in September that year notes that John Kirwan's *Milly* sailed by Paddy Cogley, beat Captain Boyle's boat.

Club Minutes of May 1930 record a decision that the regatta would be rowed over a course above the Bridges (rather than on a quay course). Perhaps a sign of a big spending burst, the committee agreed on a date for 'Regatta Purchases'. The Regatta accounts showed Catering by Love's Café of £7 and New Flags at 10 shillings. A newspaper cutting of 1931 regarding the Regatta refers only to rowing, including skiffs for ladies, despite the bad weather. By 1937 notes on the Club Regatta included 'skiff races, swimming races, obstacle races etc.'. In 1938 the club was invited to co-operate with the Town Regatta by entering a number of skiffs for a skiff race.

Seán Scallan recalled the 'fun' running this event with Murth Joyce around the late 1930s and 1940s. 'We had to go and get one of the trawlers or Murphy's big sailing boat to moor it in the middle of the river as the Flagboat, making sure to have several cases of stout on board for the men. Then we would rig up the Greasy Pole and all the other side shows'. He also recalled other times when they would sail themselves up to the Curracloe Regatta, down to the Rosslare Harbour Regatta, the Carne Regatta and the Kilmore Regatta. A later period around the 1970s was remembered by James Sinnott when he recalled the nervous lining-up of the Fireballs, as the starting gun was a live shotgun fired off the Lightship (then moored at the Quay). He remembered among the Fireball sailors, Johnnie Godkin, a Petrie and Michael Donohoe, the name of whose boat, *Nebulus Nimbus*, gave rise to some difficulties. (It was named after a cartoon character of the time). The happy ending was 'the feed of mushy peas and crubeens' in a local pub.

Programmes, 3d. each.

WEXFORD REGATTA,

Under the Auspices of the

Thursday, 7th August, 1919.

(Over a Straight Course of 1½ miles, above the New Bridge, finishing at the Boat Club).

Under the Rules of the I.A.R.U.

President:
ALDERMAN JAMES SINNOTT, J.P.

Vice-Presidents:
J. PIERCE, T. PETTIGREW, M. J. O'CONNOR, R. W. ELGEE, H. H. IRVINE.

Captain:
P. O'CONNOR.

Vice-Captain:
ALDERMAN W. H. McGUIRE, J.P.

Hon. Secretary:
J. J. GOOLD.

Regatta Officials:

JUDGES:—J. Sinnott, W. H. McGuire, J. Elgee.

STARTER:—T. Pettigrew.

CALL STEWARDS:—M. J. Kavanagh, P. O'Connor, J. R. O'Herlihy, C. J. Morris.

STEWARDS:—W. Maloney, R. Hanton, G. B. Cooke, P. Kelly, A. Lyne, P. J. Walsh, T. E. Doyle, F. Kehoe.

Admission to Stand and Enclosure - 2/-

THE FREE PRESS, WEXFORD.

SWIMMING IN THE RIVER SLANEY
must go back a long way. It is mentioned in
the Wexford Regatta Programme for July
1910 when Swimming was event No. 10 and
again in August 1919 when the Swimming
Race (Open Handicap) was listed as event No.
8. There was, up to the 1940s at least, a
public (mens') bathing place below the bridge,
down river from The Boat Club. However, as
Tom Hassett remembers, he and his family
and friends who were members of The Boat
Club (since there was 'not much other
activity in the town') would go down to the
club every day and swim across the river and
back. Sister Agnes McCormack of the
Adoration Convent grew up at the family
home on Spawell Road and remembers that
the way to swimming in the river was through
the fields below that road. She recalls Mr.
Charlie Rowe escorting his family down for a
swim early in the mornings and Hazel Rowe
Graham confirms that their father took the
boys to swim as women were not allowed. She
says that when the tide was in they would all
cycle to Ferrybank and swim around the jetty.

Swimming was rarely mentioned in the
Minutes, though in May 1934 there was a
reference to 'swimming facilities' at the club,
and to the possibility of 'getting a boat that
could act as a pontoon'. Indeed Murth Joyce
remembers around that time that they did
have an old boat from which they dived and
swam. The ability to swim in those years was

not as common as it was later, and there is a
sad little statement in the *Wexford Independent* in
July of 1898 on a drowning accident at
New Ross Regatta ending with the comment
that no expert swimmer was present.

Somewhat surprisingly, the Regatta of 1919 also
included a Water Polo event, when the
Wexford Harbour Boat Club met The Dolphins.
The competitors for The Boat Club were:
C. J. Morris (capt.), T. Pierse, A. Acres,
J. McLoughlin, P. Kelly & J. Daly, and The
Dolphins: P. Fahy (capt.), J. Pierse, W. Coe,
J. McGrath, J. Kehoe, C. J. Meagher. Mention
of Water Polo is not a frequent occurrence.

There was renewed swimming activity at the
club for a while in modern times when, about
the year 2000, the Irish Ferries shipping line
was updating its life-rafts and donated one to
The Boat Club. With some modification, this
was used by the junior club members as their
swimming base for two summers, a source of
great fun and entertainment, especially with
soapy liquids added to the water inside.

TENNIS AT WEXFORD HARBOUR Boat Club started in 1883, some years before Wimbledon! There was in the past a tennis club in Wexford off Mary Street/High Street known as the Hibernian Tennis Club and its members were known as The Hibs. It seems there was not a very large membership, mostly made up of the sacristans of the nearby churches. Melrose, or The County Tennis Club was where the Vocational Educational School now has its premises. It was known to be difficult to join Melrose and there was possibly some religious bigotry involved at times. It was a development of The Country Club, and eventually 'fizzled out' around 1954. The object of providing a tennis court at the Boat Club was originally to offer a facility for the sailing fraternity to play. It is one of the earliest such facilities in Ireland.

An article on *Social Life* in 1885 written by Fionnuala Nolan and published in the *Journal of Wexford Historical Society* gives an interesting view on the popularity of tennis. She points out that it was part of the 'civilising' influence referred to in Victorian Britain. She finds from reading Wexford newspapers of the time that 'Lawn tennis was a favourite and every comfortable house had lawn tennis courts'. She quotes Bassett in saying 'it is an active amusement in which ladies can indulge without being considered masculine, in which men may participate and yet be considered manly and which yields an excellent chance of

a good hearty romp without any accusation of romping'. The reason given for its popularity may seem amusing to us now, but it is probably true to say that the popularity and new 'respectability' of games, including cycling, skating etc. brought gentlemen and ladies much more informally into each others' presence than had been previously possible.

It appears that in 1883 the first tennis court was laid at the Boat Club venue on land obtained from the Railway Company and according to the newspapers, the first tennis tournament of the club was held in 1884.

Another tennis court was laid later on and available Minutes of The Boat Club contain very frequent and comprehensive details concerning the tennis courts and the expansion of such amenities, although not much has been found before the 1920s. A newspaper report in 1920 mentioned that 'Tennis was re-introduced over a decade ago and there are now a couple of hard courts in full swing'. According as lady tennis players began to be mentioned, Dorothy Odlum was one of the good players recalled. The lady players in particular were becoming distracted by the catcalls from passers-by on the Redmond Road - sometimes not very complimentary. It was agreed to plant a macracarpa hedge outside the courts on the railway side, and seventy to one hundred of these shrubs were to be purchased from Mr. Séamus Galvin up the road at Park Nurseries, provided they did not exceed a cost of one and sixpence each. Murth Joyce was involved in this project. In addition, wiring was erected around the courts, poles being bought from Wexford Timber Company. A tennis sub-committee was formed.

A sense of gracious living and the style of 'après tennis' refreshment is conveyed by a photograph from the 1920's.

In all the available Minute books there are frequent references to the tennis facilities from 1929 onwards. In May 1930, there was major discussion about the Upper Tennis Court and it was agreed to resurface in concrete and asphalt. However, the cost was considered too much and there was further inspection, investigation and discussion on ways and means to raise the money. It was June 1931 by the time it was decided to get the upper tennis court 'properly' surfaced and levelled with tarred screenings and chippings at a cost of about £17. This was to be paid out of club funds. Occasionally there was a big burst of spending and The club would buy a roll of netting wire for repairs to the fence around the

tennis ground. (They even bought at that time 'two dozen rough towels for use of oarsmen').

Club records of 1933 detail more active development, with Ray Corish selected to 'take charge of the tennis side and arrange matters'.

There were further experiments with The Upper Court's surface, and by May 1934 it got a coat of varnish tar. The Lower Court was also to be repaired and a means of shelter from the road considered. At the AGM of that year, a tender was accepted for four inches of concrete foundation (following digging out) and a one inch finish. This was to cost £45.

The following year it was agreed to cement the surrounds of the courts and invest in tennis poles with ratchets, and by the spring of 1936 the purchase of umpires' chairs was discussed. There was by now an active Tennis Sub-committee.

By 1937 the club had affiliated to the Leinster branch of the Irish Lawn Tennis Association and was running club tournaments. There were still only five ladies entered, though twenty men lined up to play. But rules nonetheless were strict and 'the Tennis Secretary was requested to put up notices asking the members to wear whites on the tennis courts'. In case of argument, 'The Tennis Committee shall be sole judges of what is proper tennis dress'. By the Annual General Meeting of 1937, there were reports on wiring around the courts, planting of trees and purchase of Umpires' seats - a total outlay of £54. Tennis continued to progress, and purchase of a new net was agreed in 1938. In that year there was word that the County Club was giving up its premises on Spawell Road, and there was a proposal to consider "taking over". Subsequently it emerged that the other club was not giving up as yet. However in 1939, the annual tennis tournament in The Boat Club was cancelled due to poor support.

Many local business and professional men were involved. George Bridges, whose family had a shop in Selskar, was a keen player and his ability to procure tennis balls from the shop at a time of wartime shortages, was much appreciated. (In fact taking a skiff out to recover a tennis ball from the water, is a custom that has continued - a kind of unscheduled combination of boating and tennis. As, later, an affluent society ignored balls floating out of reach, a young entrepreneur did quite well with selling the balls he retrieved). Eugene McGrail, a shop owner who opened to a late hour and was known as The Midnight Trader, was also an enthusiastic player.

The players at this time would 'tour' by bicycle, cycling off to tournaments at other clubs with the wooden racquet on the back carrier. Club member Larry Duggan remembers that there were tennis courts prior to 1930, and recalls keen players such as Ray Corish, Sean Kelly, Sandy Walsh, Jim Whelan, Frank Pettit, Paddy Kinsella, Eugene McGrail, Dick Elgee, T. Pettigrew and P. J. O'Connor, and others on the committee such as William Cullen, Murth Joyce and Frank Kehoe. Older players may also remember a character known as The Bear O'Leary.

It is clear that ladies were playing too, but the club Minutes do not give much further detail until 1949 when the annual subscription was set at twenty-five shillings for men and half that for ladies. A fund-raising tournament that year was cancelled; repairs to the court next to the pavilion were planned in April 1950 but called off as £40 was too much to spend. In 1951 however, it was again under discussion, at a lower cost, and members were to help. The trees were trimmed that year as well, and the club affiliated to the Irish Lawn Tennis Association. In 1952 the outlook was cautious; there was to be no rushing into new tennis net posts without investigation into second-hand posts.

The following year, in 1953, there were decisions to 'endeavour to get the tennis activities going'. The tree roots were by now breaking up the tennis courts but renewal had to wait until the boathouse roof was repaired. In 1955 the club decided to appoint a full-scale Tennis Committee, but no decision had been made on resurfacing the courts. A suggestion was considered to rent the Loreto courts for four months. It was agreed

J. B. and Toddy were both yachting men, and both were on the Committee of the Boat Club, but it was mainly Toddy or Tom who played tennis, a remarkable person often seen when in his seventies, setting out on his fifty year old bicycle with his bathing togs and sandwiches on the carrier as he headed for the seaside.

Players with names such as Pettit, Coffey, Corish, Carson and Whelan would treat each other to 'a round' after tennis, which meant they went to Bridges's shop for a banana or other goodies for one or two pence, or an extra treat in the form of an ice-cream which cost them three pence. This social exercise never involved any ladies - it was strictly for The Lads. The ice-cream was something of a novelty. The first ice-cream making machine in Wexford was installed by Bridges and the ice to use in the machine had to come from Waterford on the train. An indication of the work involved at the time was the fact that a man with an ice-cream cart would push his way from Selskar to The Park at Clonard on the occasion of a match, and, if he sold all his goods, he would trundle the cart back to base, restock, and push it up to The Park again!

in 1956 to go ahead with new tarmacadam and a fund-raising tournament was to be run to help finance this undertaking. The entrance fee to be 2/6d. and the proceeds to go towards the financing of the new court. Eugene McGrail presented the trophies, the tournament was a success and a new net was also approved. Around this time, the Tennis section of the club took very much more committee discussion time than the boating section. Further activity was reported a little later, in 1960, when an inter-club challenge was proposed, and seats on the court were repaired.

There are recollections of the postman Jim Morris, a keen boating man and tennis player, laying down his bag of letters on his delivery round, while he had a game of tennis in the club. Another enthusiastic player still remembered was one of the Pettigrew brothers.

Tom McGuinness, whose family have been busy club members, was an active player who contributed much to the effort to keep tennis going in the club through the 1950s and 60s.

A popular fixture still is the AUSTIN CHANNING commemorative event. Austin Channing figured so prominently in tennis in Wexford in the 1970s, 80s and 90s that it seems appropriate that into the twenty-first century a special tennis event in his name continues. Because of his views on the importance of competing as against winning, it is an unusual league run over a period of four months, through which everyone can accumulate points and everyone and anyone has a chance. His popular wife Fionnuala is also commemorated in a competition with a trophy in her name.

Austin's memo of 1972 indicates an impressive determination to revive a Tennis Club in Wexford. The aim at first was to revive Melrose Tennis Club, but this was amended to a proposal to have greater emphasis given to tennis as one of The Boat Club's activities. Proposals were made regarding the benefits of a strong tennis lobby in the interests not only of tennis but of the club, as it would be in the club's interest to have the serious tennis players enhance the club facilities and add to its social activities.

When Tom Bolger came on the scene around 1974, there was what he describes as 'a court and a half'. In 1978 the August Weekend Tournament was established, and most efficiently run by Tom and team. By the time it had been running for twenty-five years, the event had become extremely popular, attracting great numbers of players from all over the country and overseas. Popular Enniscorthy player, Dorothy Owens, described her memories of the tournament as 'always good. It was brilliantly organised by Tom Bolger who stood no nonsense from anyone. The courts were facing East/West then'. She described how her matches could be on many different courts in the area and how 'Youngsters came from all over with their gaily coloured tents, pitched by the Railway Line'. She added 'being a Granny I didn't quite fit in with the disco scene'. A former junior member describes the scene in the early days: 'At that time the Bank Holiday Tennis was mostly pretty casual and like a big family barbecue where Tom Bolger would stand on a table and announce who was playing against who, where they were going and who had a car to get them there... juniors were responsible for the BBQ and the décor, which was a bit of last year's bunting and some home-made signs. The BBQ was run by all, bringing implements and utensils from home and hoping for the best!'.

When James White joined the club in 1981, there were only about twenty playing serious tennis which soon increased to twenty-four regulars. Many outstanding players like the Kennedy family gradually became involved, and the numbers increased to ninety. In 1987 and 1988 records, there were descriptions of

Tony O'Neill, Eileen Walker, Tom Bolger, Eileen Kennedy

the courts on new reclaimed land. In 1988 the comment was that the August weekend had been "great" and the profit was £8000. By 1990 the records again showed the tournament to have been a great success with 42 courts being used by arrangement with The Boat Club. The club's own courts over the years were developed, extended, turned around and surfaced. Fencing, lighting and seating were provided, leaving the club with four fine courts.

It was in 1994 that the integration of tennis with boating was ratified in the official change of the club's name to WEXFORD HARBOUR BOAT AND TENNIS CLUB. It continues to be referred to as The Boat Club.

The Club Newsletter of Winter 2004 describes the 25th Carlsberg Wexford Open played over the August weekend of 2003 as 'another glorious spectacle'. The country's top home-based players were joined by players from Austria, France and Luxembourg, ensuring tennis of the highest calibre. It goes on to say that the Wexford Open with a Prize fund of €12,000 had become one of the highest paying events in Ireland and, with an excellent organisation team, one of the most popular among the players.

Wexford Harbour & Tennis Club

25th Anniversary

Wexford Open Tennis Tournament

PRIZE FUND €10,000
Club Phone 053 22039

Mark Channing and T.A. Walsh

Aidan and Matt Seaver

The courts before being re-positioned

Years of well organised coaching for Juniors produced results. At a time in the early 1980s when junior players were just a handful and there were two less than perfect courts, those few played all through the summer regardless of the weather, coached and helped by James McCormack. The aim was to get to the courts before the adults. In time Katherine Miller, as a qualified tennis coach, was appointed to coach both adults and juniors, and was followed by Brian Doyle and Paul Quinn. Katherine has praised Ger Hore who worked hard for the tennis players, and Kevin Lewis who organised their tournaments. In February 2004 - Osnat Manning, Tennis Captain, reports that tennis in the club is in a very healthy state with some 160 active adult players and around 100 juniors. The high standard in the junior section now, is the result of the emphasis on coaching in past years. The biggest change is the degree of activity - competitive tennis with monthly tournaments in singles for men and ladies, doubles for both, mixed doubles - senior and junior open weeks and provincial towns competitions. More people than ever are playing tennis in The Boat Club.

Ciara Pender in action

WEXFORD HARBOUR BOAT CLUB.

THE

ANNUAL · CLUB · RACES

WILL TAKE PLACE ON

MONDAY, SEPT. 19th, 1887,

OVER THE USUAL CLUB COURSE,

STARTING AT "MONTAGU'S" DEADMAN & FINISHING AT THE NEW BRIDGE.

RACING TO COMMENCE AT 1.30 O'CLOCK.

ORDER OF EVENTS.

TIME		TIME	
1.30	Senior Tub Pair-oared Boats	3.45	Junior Tub Pair-oared Boats
2.15	Scullers	4.30	First-class Four-oared Boats
3.0	First Heat Tub Four-oared Boats	5.15	Final Heat Tub Four-oared Boats

JUDGE—W. COGHLAN, J.P., R.N.R. UMPIRE—C. H. PEACOCKE, J.P.
STARTER—M. A. ENNIS, CAPT. W.H.B.C.

WOOD, TYP. 4414.

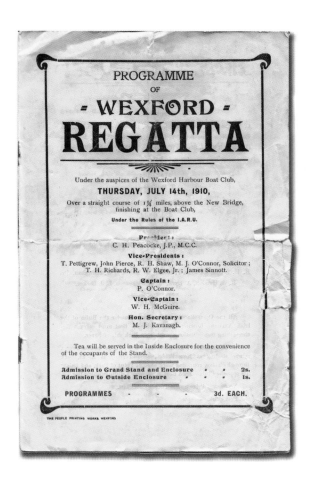

PROGRAMME
OF
= WEXFORD =
REGATTA

Under the auspices of the Wexford Harbour Boat Club,
THURSDAY, JULY 14th, 1910,
Over a straight course of 1¼ miles, above the New Bridge,
finishing at the Boat Club,

Under the Rules of the I.A.R.U.

President:
C. H. Peacocke, J.P., M.C.C.

Vice-Presidents:
T. Pettigrew, John Pierce, R. H. Shaw, M. J. O'Connor, Solicitor;
T. H. Richards, R. W. Elgee, Jr.; James Sinnott.

Captain:
P. O'Connor.

Vice-Captain:
W. H. McGuire.

Hon. Secretary:
M. J. Kavanagh.

Tea will be served in the Inside Enclosure for the convenience
of the occupants of the Stand.

Admission to Grand Stand and Enclosure - - 2s.
Admission to Outside Enclosure - - - 1s.

PROGRAMMES - - - **3d. EACH.**

THE PEOPLE PRINTING WORKS, WEXFORD

Committee Meeting 21st July, 1933.
Present:— Dr. J. E. Pierse (chairman), J. Elgee Dr. J. S. Pierse,
R. J. Sinnott & R. E. Corish (acting Hon. Sec.).
Proposed by J. Elgee, seconded by R. J. Sinnott that
" the use of one outrigger pair be given to Guard O'Driscoll
& Guard Sherlock & Cox, to practise for the Garda
Week Regatta, until the 2nd day of this regatta, they to be
responsible for any damage to Club Property, and to use
the Club premises & boat, only between the hours of
10 A.M. & 12 noon." free of charge".
Elgee
chairman 3rd Aug 1933

"MADCAP"

CERTAINLY, SIGNIFICANT SAILING had been a feature of Wexford Harbour and the Slaney Estuary from the nineteenth century. Illustrations show some of the handsome craft of the time.

By the beginning of the twenty-first century, three main categories of craft were taking part in boating activities associated with Wexford Harbour Boat and Tennis Club; Sailing Cruisers, Sailing Dinghies, and 'Other' such as motor boats.

This situation had evolved over seventy-five years. Larry Duggan thought the first sailing boats arrived at the club in the mid-twenties, and belonged to Joseph Nunn of Castlebridge, Dick Elgee, Ray O'Keefe and W. Corcoran. When it came to researching some of the assorted 'mixed class' boats of that time, informative details as well as entertaining yarns came from the old hands, past and present. These accounts may overlap to some extent. A prime example of a craft providing early excitement was Galway Hooker *The Lark* which was purchased by Tom O'Brien and Pat O'Connor in about 1938. Although these two owners have gone, many good tales have been told about the boat by others who sailed with them, such as the Fallon family, Tom Kirwan, Des McGrath and Mary O'Brien Corcoran. Even *The Lark's* voyage to Wexford was quite dramatic as she was transported from Galway to Limerick by steamship, thence up through the Shannon, and off into the Royal Canal to get to Dublin, from where she sailed down the coast to Wexford. She was painted white and had a red stripe. Once a mooring block had been made in someone's garden, she was moored close below the

'Barrelly' bridge and a little punt ferried the passengers to and fro. There were many family outings for picnics and fishing trips, the party sometimes going ashore at St. Helen's or mooring off Rosslare. Des McGrath remembers going ashore to pick cockles at "The Dairy House" and being aware that a boatload of people from The Fort had been drowned close to that point.

A really dedicated crew member was Paddy Cogley of School Street. He was the Pilot in Wexford - an old Cape Horner - a genuine deep-water sailor who had sailed in the last schooner built in Wexford, the *Antelope*. He always joined the Sunday morning outing and on one occasion they sailed down towards the harbour in morning mist which, however turned quickly into a fog. Just off the quays outside the Ballast Bank they went aground, on a falling tide with the Harbour Pilot on board. The mist cleared, and they sat there in disgrace and embarrassment most of the day to jeers and catcalls from the quayside until the tide floated them again. Padraic Fallon, poet and Customs and Excise officer, used to bring a bottle of whiskey for Paddy Cogley to enjoy, and there was an occasion when the whiskey spilled on the loaf of bread which was to be the picnic. The flavoured bread was enjoyed throughout the day by Paddy. It may be remembered that Paddy Cogley was a son of Captain Cogley of School Street, a popular man who was pilot master for 40 years and was remembered in the *Wexford Independent* of 1898. It was war time, and a regular experience was to see mines floating around them, involving sending a message to the army who would come and defuse each mine. From on board they could sometimes see sunken ships as they sailed out around Tuskar. *The Lark* had no engine, as it was removed due to the wartime petrol shortage, so all outings were under sail. Often there was a fishing trip on the business half day which was Thursday, and enough fish would be caught for several families for a week - mackerel, gurnet, and bass. Sadly this unusual vessel, (the only hooker to be painted white), which provided so much fun and fishing, ended her days beached at Rosslare when she rotted along the keel.

Paul Smyth, in his Mermaid book, lists some of the 'Mixed, unclassified boats' in Wexford in the 1940s, mentioning - as well as *The Lark* - Dr. Stan Furlong's *Niala*, Dick Elgee's *Speranza*, R. O'Flaherty's *Finola Ann*, Tom Kirwan's converted ship's lifeboat *Banba* (later bought by Seán Scallan and Murth Joyce), *Madcap* owned by Ned Hassett, and Murth Joyce and Seán Scallan's *Puffin*. The *Madcap* is mentioned under the heading of social and fundraising events. She had been owned by the Higginbothams but was won in a raffle by the Hassetts. The Hassett boys sailed her for years, including getting becalmed one night, but their parents on that occasion stopped worrying when their father went down to the Quay and it was so calm he could hear them across the water, chatting in the dark. He knew they were stuck, but alright. After too many capsizes and scares, their mother made them get rid of it!

An occasional surprise visitor came in the person of a member of the legal profession from the O'Rahilly family whose unusual mode of transport to work was to sail his boat from Dun Laoghaire to attend the Circuit Court in Wexford.

The late Raymie O'Keefe in his memoir referred to the interest in sailing in the 1930s. He added *'The Sailing Boat owners at that time were; the late Mr. John Elgee, Jack and Jim Kavanagh, Bertie Evans, the late Mr. John Martin, and a few others. The boats were unclassified and commonly known as "Pleasure Boats". Serious class racing did not appear until the Wexford Sailing Club was started in 1945 with three of the Mermaid Class Boats. This is now the strongest class in the Club. The Heron Class was introduced by Joe Tyrell in 1957 and the Enterprise Class in 1958'.*

COTS - provided something of a link between fishing, sailing and socialising and many were built by Larry Duggan. The cot has been mentioned earlier in the book, but the sailing cot could probably be described as a continuation of a type used commercially for so long in the region. Paul Smyth described her as resembling a Dory or Bank Boat and of very basic design, similar to types being used worldwide for fishing, river trade, lightering and generally making a living. He pointed out that being a flat bottomed craft, she is suited to her environment in Wexford and quite a number of them could be seen moored in the 'Cot Safe' below the bridge at the edge of the Harbour in Maudlintown.

RACING COTS - were still to be seen off the South Wexford Coast in the 1980s but the incidence of sailing cots faded after that.

As well as those included under Rowing further quite extensive memoirs were contributed by Kevin McCormack. With regret, he mentioned that in the early 1930s the adverse affects of building the sea walls at the north and south slobs were just beginning to take effect. With the changes, the scouring effect of the large volume of water was now reduced and the Harbour began to silt up. The sailing ships *Antelope, Cymric, Brooklands, Crest* and the steamships *Wexfordian* and *Menapia* could no longer be used. Yet, he remarked, there was still a ships' chandlers and still a sail loft at Maguires on the Quay. They supplied most of the stock required for The Boat Club.

He recalled that the club caretaker Dick Crosbie taught all the young chaps sail-making, how to make waxend and how to use a palm and needle. *'Around 1935'* he continued, *'another old sea dog Murt Murphy would take us young chaps out to sail. He had a wonderful craft; it captured the imagination. It was a Nantucket Whale boat capable of six knots with all six oars. He fitted a sail and centreboard. Nothing in Wexford could outsail it. When performing, his favourite expression was "Take her in by the Quay boys for a cheer" - he always got it'.*

Illustration of Whaler

Referring to the 1930s era, Kevin McCormack goes on *'There were no class sailing craft as such, merely a mixed lot of pleasure craft. Bishop Codd was of seafaring stock and had The Banshee, later handed over to Stephen Codd of Irish Lights. Ramie O'Keefe and Dr. Furlong both had ocean going craft; Tom (Jap) O'Brien had a Galway Hooker (The Lark); Mr. Rossiter had a carvel built clipper bow sailing cot Daisy Belle, Dick Elgee a fourteen foot Dinghy aptly called Speranza, solicitor Tom Kirwan a ship's boat Banba, and Patsy Meyler a very large ship's boat converted to cabin cruiser. All were moored below the wooden bridge and opposite The Bathing Place. They were scraped and cleaned and painted with anti-fouling paint at the Ferrybank'.* Before a regatta, under instructions from Dick Crosbie, they always used black lead.

'The only racing we had' Kevin McCormack goes on, *'was by necessity on handicap and at the annual regattas in Wexford, Curracloe, Rosslare Harbour, Rosslare Strand and Carne. We were all unclassified. Raymie O'Keefe and Dick Elgee expertly worked out the handicaps depending on length of craft and sail area carried. Nevertheless, not all were satisfied, and it soon became obvious we needed a Sailing Club and some class boats suitable for Wexford Harbour and coastline. After the sailing club was established, Ramie O'Keefe sold me his old ship's boat Trapper for £30. Being a student, I made it pay, bobbing for eels off Point of Park (hookless hemp catching the eels by the skin of the teeth), catching bass up near the Mile Buoy and above all fishing for gurnet out near the 'Whistling Buoy' and Oyster bed south of Blackwater bank. We would come in gutting the fish in a cloud of screaming gulls just off the breakwater to prove we were as good fishermen*

and sailors as any. We would flog the lot to Lizzie Meyler on the quay.

Dr. Hadden was the first to introduce class boats to Wexford. He was influenced by seeing so many seafaring men and youths unable to afford to follow their calling after the silting of Wexford Harbour, and compelled to swallow their pride (and the Anchor). He introduced the SNIPE class, which was relatively cheap to build. Snipe and cot races now became a feature of many regattas, but these Snipe craft were somewhat giddy and were unsuitable for any more sedate types who were not inclined to swim for it! As mentioned, it became obvious that what was needed was a Sailing Club, and then the choice of a suitable craft. The founder members of the club were Ramie O'Keefe, Dick Elgee, Seán Scallan, Kevin McCormack and Séamus Galvin (of Galvin's Nurseries). It was agreed to go for the Mermaid class, and if I remember rightly J. J. Tyrrell of Arklow was commissioned to build four Mermaids. Among the first to get delivery were Ramie O'Keefe, Dick Elgee and Séamus Galvin. I think Neville Greated built his own. The Mermaids were a hit'.

Fitting in with this memoir by Kevin McCormack is a note from Hazel Rowe Graham, recalling the 1920s and 1930s. She wrote 'In the 1930s Dr. George Hadden tried to promote a sailing club and had a number of boats made in his brother's furniture factory. He tried to sell them to people, among them the Miss Hornicks and my friend Olive Reid and me, but none of us could afford them and they were lying in the grounds of his father's house for a long time afterwards'.

Eoin Murphy remembered this too. He thought that Dr. Hadden had a vision of the water being dotted with white sails, so he proceeded to have his brother build Snipes - small dinghies which he was not successful in selling due partly to shortage of money and partly to the lack of enthusiasm of local people who had never been involved in sailing and did not understand why anyone would want a boat! His recollection was that Dr. Hadden lent them to all and sundry when they would not buy them.

Ollie Bent provided records of WEXFORD SAILING CLUB with details of all officers and Committee Members from when the club started in September 1945, up to 1964. Cecil Miller's was the signature in June 1958. This Minute book also has details of sailing race results in the 1950s and 1960s, including Cadets. He remarked that '1968 was a great year'. Earlier on there had been the Snipes, Cadets and Hornets but not all the dinghies were Class boats in the club. Eoin Murphy recalled a few Hornets. He said the Hornet had been designed by Beecher Moore who had sailed in the Americas Cup in 1934 on Endeavour. Des Tyrell said one was owned by Roy Hegarty of McCormack and Hegarty, Builder's Providers.

As part of the Club's development it is worth noting that during the mid-1950s a number of class dinghies were built by members of the sailing club section. By 1957 dinghy sailing had become very popular in the club, and this lead to the well-recorded 1958 IDRA National dinghy week with ninety boats taking part. This event was the start of a 'Dinghy Week' where all classes competed at one club. The IDRA was subsequently the IYA and then the ISA.

MERMAIDS - were probably the strongest class in the Boat Club for many years - 18 at their height. The excellent history *The Dublin Bay Mermaid* which was published by Paul Smyth in the year 2000 is a meticulous record of this class all over Ireland and is a valuable source of information on Wexford boats. When they were at their most popular in the club, the shining varnished hulls made a charming sight as the sun set above the moorings below Wexford bridge. The greatest tragedy associated with The Boat Club was the drowning in 1970 of Reverend Eddie Shearer, Rector of St. Iberius Church in Wexford, together with his crew, son Philip Shearer and a colleague Reverend Donald McLindon, Rector of Enniscorthy.

This happened when a serious storm blew up during the race for Tony O'Rourke's Cup and Eddie Shearer's Mermaid Louise was lost in horrendous conditions. As Paul Smyth wrote 'The appalling tragedy stunned the close-knit community'. There was extensive newspaper coverage, and the cloud of sadness hung over The Boat Club for a long time.

1963 Mermaid passing the remains of Barrelly Bridge

Conor Fallon, supplied some more light-hearted detail of his father Padraic Fallon's rather informal sailing around the thirties: *'My father was a great friend of Seamus Galvin....He had a Mermaid at The Boat Club - must have been among the first with ..Dick Elgee and Raymie O'Keefe - and my father used to crew for him. They both were substantial sixteen-stonish men and were unbeatable in a gale of wind - but usually last because they chatted their way round. One time they were in a race to Rosslare Harbour where they went ashore to the hotel before sailing back. My father was in oilskin dungaree trousers - then they really were oilskin - it was a very hot day - and he wore nothing under them for coolness; and pulling the boat on the sand, he split the backside of the oilskins. He brought up the rear of the party going up those old sleeper steps to the hotel and spent the rest of the day with his back to the wall...'*

Dick Ward and his Mermaid Helen

Many Mermaid sailors still belong to the club, although by the end of the twentieth century there was little or no sailing for this class in Wexford. Ollie Bent retains many of the records as does Jack Higginbotham. Jack, together with Declan Scallan, was one of the exceptionally able crew for Dick Ward, one of Wexford Boat Club's distinguished achievers at National level and the first Wexford man to win the Nationals. Another Mermaid sailor, Derek Joyce, has been outstanding in his National achievement - detailed at the end of the book. Many of the early Mermaids were built in Wexford by boat builders Neville Greated, Larry Duggan and Des Tyrell who built three each. Others were built by Johnny Ennis. Other sailors in this class were Eoin Murphy, John Corcoran, Murth Joyce, and Jim Jenkins. A story which brings a smile is the reaction of a Commodore's wife Joan who, when expressing her delight at the news of national success for a Wexford mermaid, said how wonderful it was to achieve such success "in a home-made boat"!

James Sinnott also remembers how he started in Mermaids - a leg in plaster from a hurling injury drove him to hanging around the boat club with his sister. There he got to know some of the sailors and gradually got a chance to crew in a Mermaid. He remembers a tricky event when there was a trip to Rosslare Harbour where the Mermaids were to round a mark to port and the cots to starboard, but due to some confusion there was a dramatic crash involving the Dick Elgee Mermaid!

James got a Mirror later, did some sailing in a 470 (although there was no class in Wexford) but really remained with Mermaids, and a Laser for winter sailing. He was one of those taught at the sailing classes in the club run by Brigadier Barry.

505s - This class came after the Mermaids. According to Neville Greated, Roy Hegarty got three fibreglass hulls and provided shed space through his builders' providers business. Some sails were acquired somewhere and they got going for two or three years, but never got further and David Killeen who owned one, remembers that there were not enough for competition.

FIREBALLS - A few Fireballs sailed in Wexford in the 1970s with skippers like James Sinnott and Johnny Godkin. A Fixture was mentioned in Minutes for about 1979 and an item from James Sinnott included under the Regatta chapter, mentioned lining up for a race (and its hazards).

LASERS - first appeared on the Wexford scene around the mid to late 1970s when six boats built in Waterford were bought by members of the Wexford club. David Herterich was very much to the fore and continued to promote this craft within the club. The class became popular, and the Winter Series started in the mid 1980s. Derek Joyce, who went on to Mermaid fame, was one of the club's representatives. Young sailors as they passed the age of sixteen tended to move on from Mirrors and Toppers, and sailors from other clubs like Dunmore East (more exposed to weather), took to coming to Wexford to compete in both Winter and Spring Series. Regional and National Laser Championships were held in the club, and the flying white sails on a Sunday morning became a heartening sight off the club at the wintry time of year.

LASER 2s - This is a different craft, and just a few were to be seen around the club in the 1990s.

HERONS - In notes compiled by Neville Greated he said *"Youngsters used to play poker in a dark room and were reluctant even to crew for mermaids etc.".* Neville proposed building Herons for them, with input from parents. This was agreed, and they successfully approached Ray O'Keefe for the use of a loft at O'Keefe's malt store in The Faythe. There was great co-operation also with supplies of

ENTERPRISES - Six were built for various Wexford sailors in 1958. Enterprises at their height numbered 16 or 17 and it was a lively class. David Killeen recalled that there was very close racing, and also that they had great fun; people seemed to have more free time. Among the other Enterprise sailors he remembered from that period were the outstanding Arty Corbett and his family, as well as Jimmy Meyler, Neville Greated, Brendan Corcoran, David Short and the Curtis family. One of those many enthusiasts, Dr. Barty Curtis was involved for years. As a general practitioner, he might be needed when out on the water - no cell phones then - a signal with nappy flying from Butler's window meant there was a message - two nappies meant Come back in Now! Another sailor had a signal system involving a blind pulled down in a house overlooking the water. Enterprises were built in the club during the winter in the late 1950s, under the direction of Joe Tyrell, and by 1974 the IYA Junior Training week was held in preparation for the Enterprise Nationals. The Wexford Enterprises began to do quite a lot of travelling to events at other clubs as far away as Bray and Dun Laoghaire.

timber. A sign of less affluent times came in the mention of trees being given as a gift from Pat Furlong and Herbert Zimmerman, which then had to be sawn up and seasoned before use. Herons were built in 1957, and came in for mention in the Club Minutes in 1958 when the Committee was issuing warnings about 'personal buoyancy in the Heron Class'.

GP 14s - There were some of these in the 1980s, but they did not form part of a club class as such.

FIREFLYS - This was never an active class in Wexford Boat Club, but David Killeen, who subsequently moved on to a 505 and then an Enterprise and later a Cruiser, first came to Wexford Harbour to sail a Firefly at a regatta in 1958. He stayed in a tent across the river at Ferrybank.

MIRRORS - The Mirror class, having started in a rather tentative way in the mid 1960s,

became very important in the club. George Jenkins, a keen Mirror sailor, said in reminiscing, that he was always talking with Joe Tyrell about boat building. At the time, there was not much money to buy boats. Having seen Mirror kits at boat shows, in the 1960s and 1970s, they started building them in winter at the club, working every evening from 7 to 9, both of them perfectionists. They used fibreglass stitched together with copper wire.

Before that, recalls a former member Brendan Magourty, there was the occasion when the first Mirror was displayed on the slip at the Boat Club. He was working at the time with David Noble of Wexford Creamery, and David bought the plans and built the first Mirror to appear in Wexford. In some trepidation, they went to Wexford Boat Club, carried their boat onto the premises and laid it on 'the ramparts' waiting for comment. As a meeting was just over, the Committee

emerged and Dick Elgee who was Commodore, as well as Dom Dunphy, came along with a degree of curiosity, inspecting this new boat. Its owners were told somewhat dismissively by a committee member that it was "not a class boat" to which the response was "Maybe not now - but it will be". They were indeed right, as the Mirrors grew in importance until the European Championships were held at Wexford in 1970. Before that the East Coast Championships for mirrors were also held in Wexford.

TOPPERS - The Topper, popular by the twenty-first century, is another single-handed dingy for junior sailors. It can be carried on the roof of a car and thus the six toppers in the Wexford club can travel to other venues like Blessington and Lough Erne. Most of the sailing is in the summer, and most of the national racing fleet of fifty, is based in the North of Ireland. Activities and training for the Topper class are mentioned in records from spring of 2000, and the Topper National Championships were held in Wexford in 2001. After that came something of a decline in this class.

MIRROR CLASS DINGHY EUROPEAN CHAMPIONSHIP WEXFORD SAILING CLUB TROPHY PRESENTATION & DANCE

WHITE'S HOTEL · WEXFORD
FRIDAY 31 JULY 1970
COMMENCING 8 p.m.
BUFFET · DRESS: INFORMAL
ADMIT ONE

OPTIMISTS - The Minutes record a decision in 1977 to build an Optimist in the club. However Optimists for the juniors really came into their own in the 1990s. These little boats have one sail, and are for under sixteens. Mary Kate Joyce bought one racing 'Oppie' which was raffled, raising enough money to purchase four more which were used for the summer. The best six junior sailors went on to do winter training which lead to getting on the circuit the following year. The club bought a trailer, the first 'away' Regatta was attended, and travelling for Junior sailors had begun!

Stars of the time were Derek Cowman, Ian Moriarty, Alice Cowman and Niall Dolan. Galen Lowney was another young sailor who came up through the Optimists. Many more enthusiasts followed and at a Wexford hosted regional event, there were up to 130 boats.

Ferrycarrig 1963

Winter 'frostbite' sailing as at the Wexford club, is relatively unusual in Ireland. David Killeen remembers sailing on Christmas Day. The photograph above shows the Slaney frozen over - no sailing.

SAILING CRUISERS - While cruisers had been on the scene before the dinghies, the cycle came around again in about 1975 when Brendan Swan had the first club cruiser in the form of a **LYSANDER**. His was the only one, and he allowed it to be used as a flagboat for the Officer-of-the-Day at dinghy events. About six of these were built later from kits, being double-keel, or fin. Among the owners were Jack O'Donnell, Eoin Murphy, and Angus Lee. Another Cruiser appeared when David Killeen bought one in England, and trailed it home. The complications of having to lower masts to get under the bridge led to the custom of mooring the cruisers south of Wexford bridge. This led sometimes to their skippers losing touch with the club to some extent, since their families were put aboard from the Quay and went home afterwards, the club not being very 'child friendly' at the time.

WHBTC NEWSLETTER

July 2001
Issue # 11

Newsletter of the Wexford Harbour Boat & Tennis Club

Leinster Optimist Championship 2001.

Articles for inclusion in the next issue should be e-mailed to Terry Ross at ronst@iol.ie, text may also be presented on Floppy disc, Zip disc or CD-R. Photographs of any Club activity are especially welcome and will be returned promptly.

FOR UP TO DATE BOATING & TENNIS RESULTS, AND OTHER CLUB INFORMATION CHECK OUT OUR NEW WEB ADDRESS AT http://www.whbtc.com

Another type of cruiser, the FOLK BOAT, arrived on the scene around the 1970s with Ollie Bent and Jack Devereux (with the Sherwood family) among the active skippers.

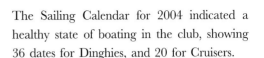

Another group moving by wind power was the WIND-SURFING or SAIL-BOARDING section. This was introduced for a few years in the late 1980s when there were about five in action, and events included Sylvester O'Brien's arrival at the club on a sailboard. It is thought that they caused a few problems for the boatman of the time, but before they gave up, the National Championships were based at the Club in 1982.

The Sailing Calendar for 2004 indicated a healthy state of boating in the club, showing 36 dates for Dinghies, and 20 for Cruisers.

UNDER THIS GENERAL DESCRIPTION are included pleasure boats, power boats, racing, and water skiing. The number of family motor boats increased steadily as more and more Wexford people took to the water for outings and picnics. Facilities for training were developed. Exploration of Ireland's inland waterways gradually became more popular. Cecil Miller, a keen enthusiast of boating on the Shannon as well as a staunch member of Wexford Harbour Boat Club, asked David Killeen to start a Slaney Branch of the Association of Inland Waterways of Ireland. This was established in 1989 with Cecil Miller as President and David Killeen as Commodore. It grew slowly until the Slaney Rally became a popular and 'fun' event for assorted boats of all shapes, sizes and classes.

By the Annual General Meeting of the Branch in 2003 there was an attendance of forty-five. A valuable contribution to boating in the Wexford area was made when Cecil Miller published the *Slaney Guide* in December 1987. It was produced with the help of a number of interested local people, including the Sea Scouts.

POWER BOATS and racing were introduced for a while. The origins seem to have been with Neville Greated and Georgie Murphy, and speedboat racing was on the agenda by October 1977. A successful season was reported for 1979. Others involved were George Jenkins and John O'Rourke. There was a Wexford Power Boat Club in 1989 and sponsors included Castrol who provided a

Cecil Miller in Calloo

valuable trophy for Driver of the Year. Long distance and circuit races were held, as well as ladies' races throughout the year. Training became available by 1992. Active enthusiasts included Jim and Caroline Boggan. The races were an exciting spectacle at the quays in Wexford. It seems to have been discontinued as it was thought to be too dangerous.

WATER SKIING - was a natural development of power boating, although Minutes mention the formation of a water skiing section as early as 1958. Neville Greated described rather basic beginnings when he built a boat from hardboard and used an old army engine, with an old surf board to ski. Kevin Lewis recalled a childhood memory of an old MG sports car belonging to George Murphy, towing a speedboat with the number X15. A pontoon was built from an oak tree which was sawn up and used with forty-gallon drums. Some negative response came from sailors about the noise and disturbance, but the Minutes record that 'the newly formed Water Ski Club be permitted to ski except when sailing races were in progress, and on the understanding that all skiers must be members of the club'. A catwalk was built at the club. The Committee did not object to the building of a catwalk. It was covered with hessian, and one man got his togs caught on a tack, and so he stood up to ski with nothing on! A junior member of those days said "I remember the skiers going off the pontoon and it was pretty spectacular when we were small".

Terry Thornton was one of the keen skiers and Peter Jeffares was also involved as were Jimmy O'Connor, Geraldine Kelly, the

McGuinness, Stones and Goggins families, Aileen Cardiff, Nicky Wallace and Ger Tighe. At one stage, the skiers became so proficient that they were able to form a 'Pyramid' which was demonstrated at Regattas. They went to West Cork to learn about jumps, and remember that in that area the skis were referred to as 'skids'. At another stage, the skiers and the speedboats would go to events on the River Shannon. On one occasion in the 1960s, for an event sponsored by Esso, free petrol was made available, resulting in a large entry of 150. Boats were smaller at that time, and did not use much fuel, but cars returned home with cargoes of assorted cans of petrol - even the drums marking roadworks were not safe from travelling boaters. Geraldine Kelly brought honour to the club when she became National Champion in Ladies' Slalom. Further up the Slaney above Ferrycarrig Bridge is a stretch of river very suitable for water skis, and the popular base for this sport moved upstream and is likely to be developed further by the McGuinness family.

A DETAILED ACCOUNT HAS BEEN written of the acquisition of land from the Railway Company at the time the club had to move across the river after the storm destruction of the first premises in 1874. An article containing all the facts relating to such dealings appeared in the *Journal of the Wexford Historical Society No.18* (2000-2001) written by the recognised authority on the history of the railways, Ernie Shepherd.

A sketch signed HG 1914, which may have been by then active member H. G. Evans, shows the basic building from the north detailing the boathouse, pavilion with curved roof, and tennis court parallel with the river. The old bridge is in the background. Many people remember it as looking exactly the same even thirty and forty years later.

Notes from a former secretary, Jim Donohoe, state 'In 1930 a new building was added beside the boathouse. This provides a gents'

changing room, toilets and a large room used for table tennis, small dances etc.' Murth Joyce described the scene about 1935 - 'the wooden bridge, the boathouse and the ladies' pavilion'. Throughout the 1930s great efforts went into maintaining the premises. The involvement included boatman Richard Crosbie who in 1930, according to the Minutes, applied for a bonus and 'was granted £5 towards a suit of clothes'. In 1935 he was retained and provided with tools for his work. The Minutes also record that in the 1930s a new Recreational Hall was added to the existing premises. Tennis was becoming very popular and the number of Sailing boats was increasing, In 1935 a "ground" committee was elected to inspect the club and report back to the Club committee.

In 1936 they became more adventurous with a proposal 'that the lawn be utilised as a clock golf course'. The caretaker was instructed to prepare the lawn accordingly and Messrs. Elverys to be contacted about the new equipment. By June 1937 the putting green was laid out, grass seed was purchased, and R. E. Corish was even directed to purchase a lawn mower provided it did not exceed £2. According to Minutes later that year "our front lawn is a credit to the caretaker and admired by members and visitors alike" and "we painted the men's pavilion and hope to do the same for the ladies this year".

In that year it was also agreed that the roof be tarred and the walls painted and supply of cushions for boats was being investigated. (Perhaps some rough behaviour had crept in, as replacement of glass in the Dressing Room was mentioned more than once in the Minutes). These references to improvements and plans seem rather at odds with an account from both Larry Duggan and Pat O'Connor which followed the mention of the rowing element having left the club in debt to the tune of £200. They said 'The Bank were putting the club up for sale so to raise funds'. The dance hall was added to the existing building in 1937 under the supervision of P. J. O'Connor of Carcur. Murth Joyce and P. J. O'Connor organised dances on Sunday nights at 2/6d per head to help pay the bills. They also acquired a cot named *Madcap*, which had belonged to Jack Higginbotham's father and raffled it to raise money.

As with most similar clubs, finance was a recurring problem. In the Minutes of 1931 there was much discussion on 'the possibility of carrying on next season'. All assets were under consideration and instructions given to collect all cups the property of WHBC which might be held in other clubs. It was around this time that there was a gap of a year in the Minute book. (Had everyone gone hunting for missing property?). In 1933 there were still "Emergency measures" in hand such as a big drive to get in subscriptions immediately. There was indeed an influx of new members, and there was also a rent on lockers. The jeweller Mr. Rudd offered to advance £20 with the trophies as security, and this enabled the Club to pay the bank £10 off the debt and ease the situation. In May 1933 it appears that the crisis had been averted.

However, things were not good in the Club by the AGM of 1939, when it was reported that 'our activities during the year were practically nil'. This was the year when a decision was made to sell the trophies. As part of an attempt at revival, a new tennis net had been purchased, the Putting Green laid out, and one Eight and one Four sold to Fermoy Rowing Club. Plans included getting 'a table tennis outfit' to be installed 'in the gents' pavilion' and a proposal was put forward to spend up to £80 on constructing a large Social Room. By 1940 there was indeed a Social Room with piano, sports equipment, table tennis, darts and 'other suitable indoor games'. Facilities were to be available to other organisations as the project had cost the Boat Club £100. Membership of the club was still falling however, having dropped over the previous four years from 105 to 89 to 77 to 76. In 1947 the Minutes recorded that in view of 'the serious financial situation of the club, it was agreed that ladies and full members be asked for an additional 25% on their membership'. The Committee managed to lodge £50 and an effort was made to pay local creditors. More fund-raising dances were to be held, a jumble sale, and possibly a fund-raising tennis tournament.

It may be as a result of recovery after the war years, that things were beginning to hum again in 1949. There was a credit in the Bank, and the position was declared to be 'most comfortable'. Membership had greatly increased, repairs were carried out and a new tennis net authorised. As far as the slip was concerned, the committee felt that 'if treated with respect, it should last a good while still', but later that year a new slip was being planned. Painting of roof and pavilions was disrupted by bad weather, but hedging to replace the trees was being considered.

In 1950, three new rowing skiffs were purchased for use by members and there were several indications of a revival and development. A new table tennis table was installed and there were further improvements to the premises. The Irish Red Cross was to be allowed to use the premises for a life-saving gala, 'provided the public did not enter the Boathouse or tennis courts'. The financial position remained shaky through 1952 when there was another attempt to sell off the old skiffs, and the sum of £5 was allocated to paint the pavilion provided the members did it themselves.

Things improved again. In 1957 there was an extension made to the slipway, repairs to the Boathouse roof were in hand, the premises being painted, and insurance enquiries ongoing (although it was 1961 before any mention of fire hose and fire extinguishers). A new lease with the Railway Company was under consideration and a decision was made to construct a dinghy park between the two slips, and the disused slip was to be renovated.

The provision of new skiffs had lead to increased use of Pleasure Boats as picnic parties could go up or down the Harbour 'where the angling conditions are ideal'. It was also recorded that 'over the past few years we have had many visiting yachtsmen from England and also from the different Sailing Clubs around the coast'. A Silver Circle was introduced to raise funds.

By 1958 there were dramatic developments. Permission was given to Wexford Sailing Club to install electricity and, with a bar now on the premises, the committee agreed to a temporary water supply as well as to improvements in the boathouse, the dressing rooms, the dance hall, the ladies' toilet and the pavilion, as well as in the boat parking area. No doubt the plumbing may not have been very sophisticated, and it was 1961 before it was suggested at Committee level that 'some kind of a flushing system for the gents toilet be considered again at the next meeting'. The slipway was rebuilt and enlarged in 1958 and described as 'one of the best slipways for sailing dinghies in the country". In further areas of development, the Sailing Club section was given the use of the Recreation Hall to build Enterprise dinghies during the winter months. The 1958 IDRA National Dinghy week event in Wexford had given all branches of the club a boost and from then on the number of boats sailing increased every year, as did the number of power and rowing boats used for water skiing and fishing. There was at this time still a reference to storing the boats 'on the tennis court in winter'. It was 1960 before a more business-like system of winter storage seemed

to come in. When David Killeen moved to live and sail in Wexford, "The Boat Club was in a tin shed and I remember the first Annual General Meeting I attended was held in a bedroom of White's Hotel".

Irene Elgee 1960

In 1961 the Minutes recorded that the entrance was to be widened and a concrete entrance way laid. Members were to give a hand with a variety of repairs and renovations. Later that year came confirmation in the Minutes "Club lawn now used as dinghy park". The lawn was put to one surprising use that year when the members of the Liverpool Philharmonic Orchestra were playing for the Wexford Festival of 1961. The Festival was a month earlier than usual, so the artists arrived in August. There was an accommodation crisis and some of the orchestra members camped on the Boat Club lawn, as confirmed by several informants. It was further reported that they were given permission to make use of the club skiffs.

As the 1960s progressed, further development occurred. The catwalk and pontoon were extended into the river for water skiing and swimming, both sections proving popular. It was agreed to purchase timbers for this job from Peter Killian who was, at the time, demolishing the old/new wooden bridge. It is worth remembering the changes in the area through descriptions from the past such as a reminder from George Bridges that originally Fortview (now the site of 1798 street) was the first house west of the town. Many people referred to 'crossing the fields' from Spawell Road, and George Jenkins pointed out that the wall between the river and the railway tracks south of the club was the railway station wall when the trains stopped at Carcur. Horse and car would take the luggage from there around Wexford.

Ground was purchased for the club from CIE, by now owners of the railway. Boat-building classes were being held in the winter. The two tennis courts were resurfaced and officially re-opened by the Mayor and reported in excellent order and well patronised. By 1966/1967 further new club premises were planned and completed as a newly formed committee had decided to build a new club house. A bar licence was purchased and the club ran dances for the several years. Reports on its value used the term 'in these days when more and more people are looking for this form of relaxation'.

From 1970 plans for development of the site continued. Correspondence shows that Seán Scallan was working hard on purchase of extra land from CIE. In 1973, in the Sailing Club at least 'the fiscal state was good'. In a major change at the premises, from having no water, the club had moved to a smart bar. In

1976 it became necessary to issue a reminder of the dress code in that no more wet suits and oilskins could be worn in the bar. In 1977 and 1979 two new slips were laid. In 1978 the Boat Shed was erected by Duggans at a cost of £1,700.00.

Over the years the maintenance and development of the premises arose frequently in all recorded discussion and in valuable notes from former Club Secretary Jim Donohoe. In 1979 more plans for development were under consideration and building work was under way again in 1983 when the old downstairs bar and kitchen were demolished and a new entrance and stairs erected by Duggans by 1985. Mention of the stairs brings back memories for one sportswoman; "After Junior Boating, to get a lift home we used the old black Button A & B phone by the stairs in the club. We would have been given 10 pence between three or four of us for the call. At some time someone worked out how to make the call and get the 10 pence back, using Bluetack or glue, and a piece of thread. Ten pence got ten Fizzlesticks...".

The next phase in development of the Premises was in 1989 following condemnation of parts of the building by the Fire Officer. There was a jetty extension in that year and a new flagpole. There was also a new Snooker table purchased for the Snooker Room for £1100. In 1991 came a decision to raise a loan of up to £20,000 and in 1992 further building was carried out on the premises, and the extension opened in 1993.

Meanwhile, a major innovative proposal to move the entire club premises to a new venue at the former Clover Meats site at the south end of Wexford town was investigated thoroughly, and an elaborate proposal put to an extraordinary general meeting at the end of the eighties. The proposal, which was spearheaded by John Scallan, arose from the limitations at the present site, because of the railway, the silting up of the estuary and other difficulties. The decision, influenced by the views of the club's trustees, was not to move. Following this decision, the existing jetty was extended, and further negotiation was instigated with CIE regarding availability of land, and repairs to, or replacement of, the bridge over the railway line. This deal, including replacement of the bridge, was completed in 2003, by which time there was extended dinghy parking covering .8 of a hectare and well lit tennis courts, helping with all-year-round use of both tennis and boating facilities. The total area of the club was gradually and slowly extended over the years, both through extensive reclamation work, and acquisition of property from the railway company. Negotiations were often slow and frustrating, not helped by the fact that the boundary of Corporation and County Council ran through The Boat Club property. A large part of the east end of the new tennis courts was reclaimed land and the total area of the club grew to some 1.6 hectares.

An exciting development at the end of the century was the arrival of the pontoon which was purchased after its use in the filming of the Spielberg movie *Saving Private Ryan* during a summer at Curracloe and Ballineskar. Also, in the year 2000, the east and west wings in the club building were refurbished and a new bar installed by Duggans.

An essential part of the use and development of The Boat Club premises must be the story of those valuable personnel who have worked there over the years. These have included bar staff, managers, boatmen and caretakers. In particular, many people talked about Dick Crosbie, employed as boatman/caretaker for some twenty-five years from around 1926. He was held in high regard and tributes came from many former club members such as Neville Greated. Kevin McCormack expressed his admiration well; 'The caretaker Dick Crosbie was for us young chaps the main attraction of The Boat Club. He was a father figure - an old sea dog'. He is mentioned in the Sailing chapter, and had been a schooner skipper of *The Wave*.

Tommy Pender and Dessie Byrne

There were other boatmen and caretakers such as Bill Morris, Jack Higginbotham, Phil Swan, John Meagher, Dessie Byrne, Ray Wickham, Tony Furlong, Tommy Pender, Sylvester O'Brien and Philip Hatton. The Caretaker's Hut became something of an institution and served many purposes. At one stage it was known as 'Castelgondolfo', being Tommy Pender's 'Summer Residence'.

Tommy Pender

By 2004 the position was held by Roy Warner and other popular bar personnel were Freda, Brendan and Pat.

DREDGING

Silting up has been a continuing problem. Declan Power, an oarsman with Ferrycarrig Rowing Club, as well as mentioning that the Boat club had at times been used as a stage in long distance races from Ferrycarrig, also recalled that he had on two occasions dredged the area near the club. Using a barge with a digger scoop on front, he would remove mud to leave a depth of three metres of water.

Eddie Ferguson also remembers dredging around the slip, using club boat *Bay Searcher* which came from Pembroke and required considerable investment and attention at the Wexford club ('More money spent on her than the *Titanic*' said a former club treasurer). Eddie Ferguson has described her as definitely 'a general purpose workboat', since she has seen duty for laying moorings, as a committee boat, as a ferry during the filming of *Saving Private Ryan* and for dredging with the installation of a specially adapted arm, at

The Bay Searcher

which time she became known as *The Back Scratcher*. Dredging at the club by Declan Power was carried out once again in 1992 at a cost of £1000.

When referring to 'special' boats, the Miller barge must be included. *Knocknagow* was originally a barge based in Carrick-on-Suir, was sailed around the coast to her new home near Enniscorthy and reincarnated as a Roadstone dredger in use higher up the Slaney. Years later in the 1970s, she was bought and converted back to a barge by Richard Miller and for years was on hand on many occasions in many capacities including that of "Toilet Boat" for Junior sailing events. Much nostalgia was aroused with her sale in 2004.

Some other surprising craft have been associated with The Boat Club premises. In particular there was something of a love/hate relationship with an odd workboat of non-specific design, which became known as The Tin Can. She sank so often that it became

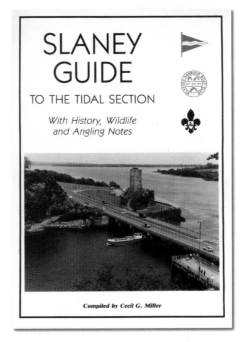

Knocknagow at Ferrycarrig

a regular occurrence for club members to wade out over the mud, bail her out and make some changes to the engine and off she would go again!

Derek Joyce's Zuleika

Any mention of 'special' boats at time of writing this book must include *Zuleika*. Paul Smyth, in his book on Mermaids, has this comment on her first appearance: '...*the arrival in 1996 of Derek Joyce's Zuleika No. 187, which was built by Des Tyrell of Wexford and launched at the June Bank Holiday weekend. She at once returned a series of staggering performances and it was immediately evident that this Mermaid was something special, nothwithstanding Joyce's undoubted helming skills. At the National Championship in Skerries the same year, she proved to be unbeatable, taking five first places, giving her an unassailable lead...*'.

Derek Joyce and *Zuleika*, having won five races in the Nationals in 1996, went on to come First again in 1997, Second in 1998, First in 1999 and Second in 2000. Bringing honour to Wexford Boat Club's reputation, Mermaids built by Des Tyrell came First, Second and Third at the National Championships in Fenit in 1998.

CRANE - The crane in use to lift boats at the club was purchased from the South Station. This crane was historic in its own way as it was installed for the main purpose of lifting machinery from Pierces and from the Star Foundry. Richard Miller gave details about the special steam lorry with two wheels at the back and one in front to allow for the turning. The crane was bought for £5 (€6.30) and was sold in 2003 for €500 so it was apparently a good investment! The crane purchased in 1976 was dismantled at the North Station by Larry Duggan, Dessie Byrne and Tony O'Rourke. In 2003 a new crane was purchased from Howth Yacht Club through the efforts of Philip Scallan.

CHANGING ATTITUDES AND THE SOCIAL SCENE

ANY CLUB OR ORGANISATION existing for one hundred and thirty years will reflect social change. The Boat Club is no exception. The earliest memory we could find came from Hazel Rowe Graham in 2002 when she was over ninety. *'The Boat Club'* she said, *'was, I think, very popular about the turn of the last century when my parents were young. My father often spoke of it and their excursions upriver to Ferry Carrig and so on for picnics with lots of friends. We also found mention in papers of Harry Rowe, my grandfather's young half-brother, as a member in about the 1880s'.* (It is worth noting that the grandfather in question was former Mayor of Wexford Howard Rowe, the miller). Hazel added *'In my time the club didn't seem to be so popular'.* That would have been in the 1920s.

For many years in the twentieth century there was a perception that The Boat Club was elitist and "snobbish". Murth Joyce called it rather "West Brit" in the early part of the century and the prejudices and politics were probably in keeping with attitudes of the time. Indeed it is remarkable to read in Minutes and Rules that ladies and juveniles were not allowed on the slip, and that the system of becoming a member included not just a proposer and a seconder but also consideration by the committee, which sometimes turned down the application. It would appear that the infamous 'blackballing' however, though sometimes still mentioned in 2003, applied not to the Boat Club, but to the Tennis Club at Melrose. There are people who remember that even in the 1940s *'lads from Parnell Street and William Street, when rowing up the river from the town, would cross the river to the east bank on their way up to the Point of Park in order to avoid rowing across the water near the club in case they might be summonsed'.*

Juveniles had no rights early on, and restrictions were mentioned in the club Minutes. In 1933 the Committee agreed that there should be no children 'at all' on the premises, and in 1937 came a reinforcement of the rule that no person under the age of 16 years could be admitted a member of the Club, but over 16 they could be on the family ticket. By 1948 a Minute says that the minimum age for Juveniles was to be ten years, and then in 1953 at a time when the list of Juveniles was closed in May, it was agreed to admit, as vacancies occurred, up to 30. By 1958 the rules about times of attendance in the club were relaxed to allow for playing tennis. However, in much later years, there came a time when there was a very short-sighted policy of discouraging young people from the club. After the 1960s came a

Included in this elegantly clad gathering are: Mrs. Edwards, Dorrie Pettit, Rita Donohoe, Anna Lambert, Mary Sherwood and Peg Sherwood.

period when sailing classes petered out, and there was nothing for young sailors. By the time new social activities started to develop in the club, in the 1970s and 1980s there were only six young people there to help. Such a 'demographic gap' has a serious and depressing effect in any club, as inevitably there will be no new members coming through, and it took until years later to get young peoples' activities really going again in Wexford Boat Club.

The situation for Ladies was even more dramatic. This, said John Sherwood, was originally a Gentleman's Club. Ladies were not allowed on the slip, they were not allowed to attend meetings, and they were not allowed in boats unless escorted by a competent gentleman. Sister Agnes McCormack (now of the Adoration Sisters in Wexford) and her sister were taken out in their youth by District Justice Fahy, and that was alright. On 10 April 1935 'An application by the Ladies for an extension of use of the club was quashed'. They did pay a membership subscription, but in that same year 1935 when the fee was being increased by 5/-, it was agreed by the

committee that only half the amount was to be 'put on the women's sub.' and it was decided to circularise the ladies for subscriptions before they could be admitted to club premises.

When in 1939, it came to a meeting to organise an innovative Gala Opening Day for the new Social Room, five ladies were allowed to attend the meeting to organise the event. From then on, ladies were to the fore in all catering and organising functions. In 1940 there was a club excursion with 'a picnic tea to be served by the ladies'. Again in the minutes of 1947 comes a committee suggestion for a picnic, and 'a Ladies' Committee is formed to deal with catering matters at the dance afterwards'. Ag Corish, whose husband was an excellent tennis player, recalls that "the Ladies always made the sandwiches".

It was however, noticeable that they did not yet have equal status. Obviously feeling was beginning to run high in 1952 when at a meeting 'Mr. A. Cadogan's remark that "it had not been worth electing a Ladies' Committee" caused a stir! 'At this point a number of members started speaking loudly together and the Chairman had to call the meeting to order. He said that the fault lay in having not appointed a secretary to the Committee.'

In 1958 records show that the subscription for Ladies was 15/-, but clearly this did not solve all problems, because at the Annual General Meeting of April 1959 an application was considered for permission for the ladies to swim or water ski from the slip 'but as there was a rule forbidding this, nothing could be done about this request'. Restrictions began to relax in 1960 when the committee introduced an 'amendment to club rules to permit Lady Members of the club to wear bathing dress when water skiing from the club premises. Bathing attire not to be worn on the tennis courts..' The subsequent importance of the club's lady members is highlighted further down.

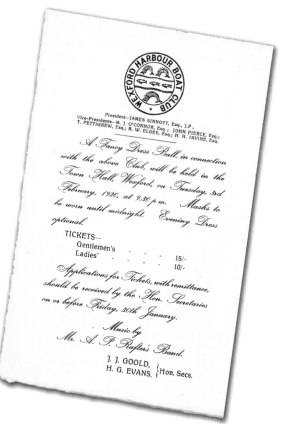

While the Boat Club had long been the venue for restrained and refined social activities, over the years it gradually became the scene of more ambitious, wide-reaching and lively events.

In 1931 the Committee went so far as to give permission to run tennis tournaments on boat club courts in aid of the Adoration Convent Bazaar, and there was a year when a Fancy Dress Dance was held in the Redmond Memorial Hall. In 1933 the committee again made some decisions on Social Events, when it was decided that Teas were to be allowed in the Gents' Pavilion in case it should rain on days when other events were postponed. An ironic note came from someone who said the ladies brought along their silver and china for the Teas, but there was still no running water laid on, and water had to be conveyed in buckets by volunteers who would cross through the fields to Bradishes at Strandfield on Spawell Road. (It was the only well that did not run dry in the drought of 1940).

Another big decision at that time was 'To allow a club dance on occasion if proper control be used and no abuses be allowed to creep in'. The Teas must have lapsed because in the committee minutes of 1937 there is mention of Revival of Teas on Sundays and Thursdays, as well as the Revival of informal club dances in the Pavilion. This seems to have been a year when everything was more lively, including the Regatta and a variety of skiff races and rowing events and even 'obstacle races'. Indeed by 1938 it was announced that the club was once more solvent and the secretary T. J. Kirwan expressed gratitude 'to the committees who over 4 to 5 years had turned a practically bankrupt concern and achieved this splendid result'. Rules were strict; no racing boats, the property of the club, were allowed to leave the boathouse on Sundays. In 1939 the proceeds from the dance were £7.15. Many years later, the dance only yielded £1 in profit!

There must have been a good relationship with other organisations, as amenities and facilities were often shared and help given for example to The CYMS and the Christian Brothers School, and attempts were made not to clash with events being run by the Hockey Club and the Feis. Later there was co-operation with other groups such as Civil Defence, the Harbour Commissioners, an on-and-off relationship with Hockey Clubs, and lease of premises to a Bridge Club.

Hard times came round again. Not long before his death in 2002, the late Pat O'Connor of Carcur gave a verbal account of his recollections of the club which he joined in 1938. He figures in many of the old photographs as for example sailing the *Madcap.*

He recalled those hard times around 1949 when the club owed the Bank £260 and was to be closed down. In the effort to raise funds, a sailing dinghy *Madcap* was raffled. To boost sales, she was sailed up and down near the club to draw attention to her worth. The money raised on that project was invested in a building extension to run fund-raising dances. As there was no electricity, a single 15 watt bulb, run off a car battery, provided light for these occasions. Whenever the lighting system failed, the dancers were not displeased,

but in time there was a complaint from the clergy about the immorality of it all.

There have been many smiling recollections of The Boat Club Dances. George Bridges remembered in the late 1940s and early 1950s organising collection of the 1/- at the entrance to the Hut. He said that the Band consisted of Peter Doyle on melodeon with a drummer and another musician. They were paid 5/- and a bottle of stout, plus transport. Dances were run for many years; Marie Fane remembered "everyone walking or going by bicycle, and all the staff from Hadden's shop going in a group". Hadden's was later Shaw's. David Killeen remembered the dances as great fun; Nicky and Mairéad Furlong used to attend too.

There was a period when attendance fell off, and there were only three people on one occasion, so there was new discussion and debate about running dances in the Golf Hotel in Rosslare and one in the Town Hall in Wexford. There was some more new thinking, innovations like a Gala Opening Day for a new Social room, and an excursion to Dunmore and Tramore in two buses. In a further effort it was agreed to raise funds for the purchase of a piano at £8. Teas were to go up from 6d. to 1/-. An excursion *with picnic* was planned at an inclusive cost of 10/- which covered the dance in the Atlantic Ballroom in Tramore. One wonders about the picnic menu, as the committee agreed 'a quotation to be got from Miss Mernagh for sauce'... In 1940 there was another club excursion - not by bus this time - as 'the boats were to leave at 1 o'clock for the picnic'. By 1941, the committee went so far as to agree that the use of the club could be given to a charitable organisation for one day only during the season.

In 1947, several things happened. Club dances were under way again, and an Amusement Secretary was appointed in the person of the sailing, tennis-playing, singing postman, Jim Morris. Then came a decision to purchase table tennis bats, but alas then the club was found to be in an overdraft situation once again. Complaints were coming in about 'crashers' refusing to pay their entrance fee to the dances, there was insufficient co-operation to hold a jumble sale, so then it was decided to have a 'band benefit dance' in the pavilion.

In May 1948 there was to be a day's outing to Courtown but this time members with cars were to be asked to provide transport. Dances must have been going well again, as it was agreed the band should get a raise of 6/- as applied for. The following year the dance subscription was raised by fifty per cent and there was much more reference in the Minutes to social activities, there was an Open Day with golf competition, darts competition and swimming races. For the first time there was mention in the Minutes of the club flag. There was a picnic to the Saltees which Murth Joyce remembers. 'Tourists' and 'temporary members' were to pay a set fee. There were lots of new members, the caretaker got a raise, there were more dances, and a humourous paper went into circulation, *The Slimey Slip*, largely the work of Seán Kelly and Sim Hore. Joe Lowney confirmed that he was one of those who provided dance music.

Once into the 1950s, social events were more ambitious. The Open Day that year included an American Tournament, Tea in the pavilion, Rifle Range and Gala Dance. The Sailing Club was to hold two races, and a small band was to play on the lawn during the evening. In 1955, the dances were in the Redmond Hall (near the present-day Redmond Park) and then in 1960 the Monday Night 'Hops' were being continued in the club. The Juniors were to have 'gramophone hops'. It was decided not to hold dances in the Town Hall because of competition with the new Dun Mhuire Hall in the Main Street. It is ironic that much later the popularity of Wexford's Centenary Stores put an end to the very popular, and financially successful discos which flourished for about ten years in The Boat Club. It had been a significant phase in the long history of more than a hundred years of schemes to raise money for the club. Events were not all frivolous, as records show a period of 'Lectures' held in the club.

At one stage in the late twentieth century a popular annual event in the Boat Club was the day when the Maudlintown cots would come up to race at the club. The cotmen, skilled in manoeuvring by shifting ballast, would sail to upstream of the area around the Point of Park, and fill their sand bags to be ready for the racing. It was a family occasion, the children would all be entertained, the band played, everyone was provided with refreshments, the men raced the cots, and women brought their knitting. Perhaps also in the 'Social' category, would be a mention of Larry Duggan's boat *The Bar* or *"Gigfy"* acronym for Guinness is Good For You! This event has died out. However a buzz of different social activities developed at the club, including the discos (Junior and Senior), barbecues, Santy's visits by boat and helicopter, bar extensions, and the entertainment of the Tennis Weekend.

Meantime the intrepid bands of ladies who catered for functions and worked so extraordinarily hard made rather a mockery of the rule about no Full Membership for Ladies, even though they were certainly appreciated when it came to catering. Eventually, in an age of equality, the women were finally classified as Adults. Callista Murphy remembers all the work for the women, with the borrowed Burco, the sandwich making, the dinners for sailors and all with restricted facilities unlike the streamlined quarters of today. Back in 1969 Mary O'Rourke was the key figure in the development of catering support as well as other social activities in the club. She was first chairman of the newly formed Ladies' Committee, with Sylvia O'Connor as Honourary Secretary. The records of this Committee give some idea of the practical approach. They gave thought, not just to numbers, but to new curtains, to availability of the Caravan Park across the bridge, loan of delph and cutlery, the

preparation of the stew by Mrs. Ward and her team, the how, where and what of the vegetables, sandwich-making, and finally the Washing Up. The formation of this committee, through the Sailing Club, was prompted by the Forthcoming Mirror Championship of 1970. Mary, involved at a time when her husband Tony was captain of the Mermaid class, remembers when the catch phrase was "Friday Night is Boat Club Night" because of the social activities. She was one of many who kept things going behind the scenes and all her colleagues are listed in the records.

Taoiseach Jack Lynch, Maureen Lynch and Cecil Miller

The Club has welcomed some quite special visitors at different times. Among these was the 1970s visit of RNLI HopeRoberts when there was barely enough water at the slip as she motored in for official launch by Maureen Lynch, wife of Taoiseach Jack Lynch.

When Wexford 'twinned' with the Breton coastal town of Coueron in 1982, flotillas sailed to and fro between the two places. A look at Eddie Ferguson's scrap book for the

years 1991 to 1996 reveals many messages of thanks to club members, from boat crews, not only from around Ireland but from Scotland, Wales, England and France. There is special appreciation of the hospitable welcome in Wexford and assistance by way of marker buoys and pilots from the club. Boats include the *Happy Cat* on her way to the West Indies grateful for the escort through Wexford Harbour. The visit on October 6th, 1994 of the Sail Training Vessel *ASGARD II* was a very important occasion. She was the deepest vessel to arrive in Wexford Harbour for years, and getting her across the harbour bar and up to the Quay required special help and co-operation from Wexford Harbour Boat Club which was greatly appreciated by skipper and crew.

A special event in 2003 was the club's participation in the excitement of the transport of the torch and torch-bearers for the Special Olympics held in Ireland that year, when Wexford was host to Poland, and club boats made a striking contribution to the ceremonies while part of the team was in Wexford.

Asgard II

Socialising in the club

UNDER THIS GENERAL TERM COMES a wide range of learning activities for young and old. At the beginning of the twenty-first century, the club has been described as like "a little university" in wintertime. Coaching for tennis players has taken place over the years and is covered in the Tennis chapter. Formal sailing classes had their good and bad periods. In the 1960s there was a time when young people benefited from the teaching of committed, experienced and highly respected sailors like Arty Corbett ('so particular he carried a little pot of varnish with him when out sailing'). The enthusiastic retired Brigadier John Barry who moved to Rosslare from England with his wife Mary gave great service as a teacher at The Boat Club with the help of the popular Felicity Poole.

There was that blank spot around the 1970s when sadly, attention to young mariners was ignored. This meant that people born around the 60s 'missed the boat' as it were, and later teachers have said there was 'almost a generation missing' and 'no new blood'. Even later when the attitude had changed once again, an unsympathetic older member was heard to say disapprovingly "Look at the state of the place - all children and dinghies!". However this atmosphere did not last long. Courses were later run by Des Tyrell and Derek Joyce, and also by Jane Kelly. Mary Kate Joyce arrived from Skerries with great

Felicity Poole

enthusiasm and persisted until she got classes under way for junior sailors and got the ISA involved. Courses became popular and well attended for both Juniors and adults, and the club, as well as the 'Junior Organiser' is very busy in July as courses are attended by up to sixty. These young sailors are from Wexford and elsewhere, the visitors becoming temporary club members. The course covers various levels up to that of Instructor, and young qualified Wexford instructors can teach at home and then go away for experience to such destinations as Greece, the Caribbean and America.

Among the young mariners to reach a crowning achievement in competition at national level were Van Maanens, Niall Cowman and Louise Kerr. James Sinnott continues Laser coaching.

Race Officers courses are run by Des Tyrell with Navigation Courses under the ISA scheme running for many years under the direction of Mike Doyle and Phil Cowman. David Sherwood through the Department of the Marine, became a licensed instructor and examiner for Marine radio-telephone. In 1999 a Power Boat Instructors' Course was initiated with external instructors at the start. In 2000, under an ISA scheme, David Maguire and Peter Scallan were sent to train as instructors. Courses were subsequently run by the Club to Advanced Level and the International Certificate of Competency offered. In winter, another course run in the Club is in First Aid, and there is even a Wine Course.

In the winter, the Wine Development Board of Ireland ran a series of Wine Appreciation evenings attended by twenty two boaters and tennis players. Sampling everything from wines off the supermarket shelf to what they described as 'Classy Champagne', the club members learned about wine from different countries and different grapes. It was a new and enjoyable form of 'tuition' and considered 'all good fun'.

Youngsters developing their sailing skills

Sarah Duggan and Louise Kerr

FINE TROPHIES HAVE BEEN presented over the years for many of the club's competitions in both tennis and boating. When rowing had been discontinued as a club activity, and the club was short of money, it was decided to sell a number of the rowing trophies to Rosslare Golf Club. The fate of the trophies arose frequently in discussion at Committee meetings according as the club finances went up and down.

In 1939 valuation was being procured with a view to selling trophies to Mr. Richards. In the summer of 1940 they were sold to Rosslare Golf Club. It was obviously a formal transaction involving considerable negotiation. The sum of £35 had been mentioned originally by The Boat Club, and The Golf Club had been authorised to go as far as £40, but in the end the amount which changed hands between the clubs was £27.10. Unfortunately a number of these trophies were subsequently stolen in a golf club robbery.

Many long established trophies remain in existence with The Boat Club and competitions for them continue to be run annually. An entry in Rule Books states 'Any cups won by Boats belonging to the club to be the property of the club' and from time to time it has been suggested that the committee draw up a full register of the trophies.

To some extent the trophies reflect the outstanding people who were members of the club in different categories and different eras. Among these are the Richards Trophy which became the O'Connor Cup. This fine trophy with oarsman on top must have been a Rowing Cup when originally presented by Tommy H. Richards in 1903. Having been 'won out' by Reverend Tom O'Connor, it was later reactivated by his brother Fintan O'Connor in 1961 and presented by him back to the Boat Club, this time as a Sailing Trophy for the race to Carne (where Fintan O'Connor had a house, and therefore a special interest).

There is the Tony Jacob Memorial; Tony Jacob is remembered not only as a fine sailor, but also a tragic figure. He was one of the Jacob family of Rathdowney, Rosslare and sailed the cutter *Ituna* to America and back in the 1950s. Sadly, after he made a second voyage to America to deliver another craft, at a time when he and his companions were setting out to train as architects under the American Frank Lloyd Wright, Tony Jacob contracted polio and died. After that initial American trip and before Tony's sad death, *Ituna* was raffled through Irish Sweeps and won by Redclyffe Yacht Club, after which it was delivered by Cecil Miller of Wexford, and a crew which included Richard Elgee as well as Mr. Frank Jacob.

A handwritten account of the trip has survived, and some of this is reproduced below:

'When in Wicklow, Mr. Frank Jacob was washing his dentures and unfortunately dropped his uppers overboard. Tony, his son, dived for 15 minutes but failed to recover them. Mr. Jacob also was a bad sailor and was very seasick for 15 hours. When off Tuskar, it was my trick for three hours, but it was wonderful sailing and I stayed on for 4 hours. The sea was all phosphorous and the waves were sparkling and the log trailing astern was sparkling like a firework. Tiller lines were used in a strong breeze. We used a big square sail which Tony had used on his Atlantic trip. We had no engine so all manoeuvres were done under sail. Ituna was thirty-six feet long and a twelve and a half ton cutter. This trip took about ten days.

Following fog and then strong north-westerlies, the weather cleared and we had good sailing - main and genny. Picked up Pendon Light, passed outside Longships, entered Penzance. Dropped hook off pier as harbour dries out. After visit ashore, embarked again and sailed to Newlyn harbour and tied up outside Lutin, a French boat. The Frenchmen very friendly. Departing in strong north westerly, very excellent gybe in harbour to clear pier and set course for Lizard. Friendly waves from Lutin anchored outside.... Passed Eddystone Light, weather improved, wind moderating, abreast Plymouth 19.15. Picked up Bolt Head 22 hours and entered Salcombe in darkness - rather tricky. Dropped hook. Criscraft came alongside and towed us into more sheltered water. Squadron Leader Payne and Swiss Miss came aboard for drinks. ... Salcombe a lovely spot. Went dancing. Left Salcombe for Torquay Sunday. Sunshine and showers, good breeze and running with tide. Wind got strong. Entered Torbay in rough sea, shipped a sea into genny and it tore. Got thoroughly wet. Sailed into Torquay, had poor dinner at Mayflower and went to pictures, Alice in Wonderland, V.G. Comfortable night. 13 Aug. Left Torquay for Tynemouth. Becalmed. Off with square sail. Lovely red cliffs. Put into Babbacombe and went up cliff in funicular railway.

Departing, set course for Lyme Bay buoy and Portland. Lots of traffic around Shambles - took over from Richard (Elgee). Entered Swanage and dropped anchor. The Centurian came and dropped anchor seventy yards away (great excitement) Cleaned up Ituna. Everything A1.. Drifted towards Poole. Picked up by M.V. Turin and towed up to Wareham via Poole. Changed flags and then off up narrow River to Yacht Club. Received with 7 gun salute and returned same by Verey Light. Frightened some cows.'

Records include a very gracious letter of thanks from the new owners at Redclyffe Yacht Club.

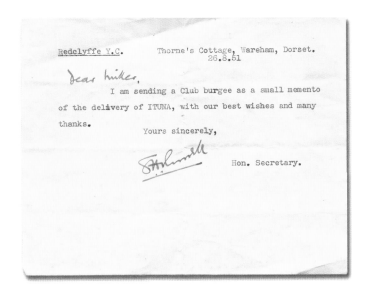

Redclyffe Y.C.   Thorne's Cottage, Wareham, Dorset.
                            26.8.51

Dear Miller,

    I am sending a Club burgee as a small memento

of the delivery of ITUNA, with our best wishes and many

thanks.

                Yours sincerely,

                                Hon. Secretary.

More Boating trophies include the Butler Cup, the Slaney Challenge Cup, the Menapia Challenge Cup, and the Ray O'Keefe Memorial Cup as well as the Sherwood Cup and the Zimmerman Trophy amongst others. An unusual trophy is a miniature Mermaid model won outright by Eoin Murphy.

A curiosity among club trophies is a wooden tankard with pewter insert. This was found at auction and presented to the club by Frankie O'Driscoll and then meticulously repaired by Des Tyrell. The Tennis section similarly reflects the memory of distinguished players in the names of the trophies.

AS COMPETITIVE SAILING DEVELOPED there was a need for club rescue facilities to provide safety cover for club and open racing. Until the 1970s the mainstay of the rescue fleet was the club workboat supported by members' motor boats. Larry Duggan was commissioned to build a replacement for the existing club workboat in 1976. She was built in O'Keefe's loft where the 6 Herons were built. This 21ft. clinker-built launch powered by a Lister inboard diesel engine was initially known as *Rescue 1* (or The Workboat). Upon the arrival of the Bay Searcher in the mid 1990s *Rescue 1* was renamed *River Searcher*. Both *River Searcher* and *Bay Searcher* have always been painted in the club colours of red and white.

In the 1980s the club rented and borrowed rigid inflatable boats (or RIBs) for major events and eventually purchased a RIB of its own in the late 1980s. This was subsequently joined by others, and by 2004 the club had a safety boat fleet of five boats.

The availability of private boats, and latterly the club safety boats, meant that in the case of an emergency on the river Slaney or in Wexford Harbour the first option of An Garda Siochána has always been to call the Boat Club and the Sub-Aqua Club. In 1976 there was already discussion in the club about the need for further rescue facilities.

This came to a head after a number of accidents and drowning incidents in the mid - 1990s. The then Vice-Commodore Eddie Ferguson organised emergency equipment and twenty-four hour availability of the club RIBs.

He sought advice from Water Safety Ireland who made a series of recommendations. It became apparent that public rescue facilities were not generally within the scope of the club. A number of club members and others within the community, led by Eddie Ferguson, established a special community inshore rescue station under the auspices of Water Safety Ireland. After about two years of planning, it got going in 1997.

A second-hand 'D' Class Inflatable Inshore Lifeboat was purchased from the RNLI and renamed the *Paddy Busher* in memory of a drowning victim who was a member of a well-known Wexford family. A temporary building was procured and located on The Boat Club grounds. In 1999 Wexford Inshore Rescue became a Declared Facility of the IMES (Irish Marine Emergency Service), later renamed Irish Coastguard. (Years earlier, there had been somewhat primitive Coast Watch services around the coast, involving the firing of the Breeches Buoy as remembered by Sylvester O'Brien).

The station from 1999 was run on the lines of an RNLI Inshore Lifeboat Station, with some training provided by the RNLI and Water Safety Ireland. The RNLI took over the station in 2002 and added to the temporary buildings. The first RNLI boat on station in Wexford Harbour since 1927 was the relief D Class Lifeboat, *D469 Winifred and Cyril Thorpe*. The Club celebrated the return of the RNLI to Wexford Harbour by hosting a Midsummer Ball in the Talbot Hotel in June 2002. It was a memorable and entertaining night organised by Ruth Coulter and Des Tyrell on behalf of the club.

By 2004 there were 16 crew and 7 other personnel attached to the station, backed up by a fund-raising team led by Mary Doyle and Eithne Coulter. A weekly exercise programme was established for boat and crew, and launch on service was required approximately 10-15 times per annum.

There were many spin-offs from the co-location of the Inshore Rescue Station with the club. These included greater safety standards, e.g. life-jackets, better boat maintenance and preparation. The development of both Powerboat Training and VHF training were a result. Communications also improved dramatically with the result that the Radio Communication courses were run and VHF radio licences awarded to qualifying members. Club equipment was upgraded. The situation represented a considerable change from 1873 when *The Wexford People* contained a news item stating that at New Ross on July 12th a sailor off a schooner 'accidentally fell into the water and was drowned. Captain Walsh, the Master, offered one pound to any person who would recover the body, but it was not found until it floated on the 18th...'.

WHAT IS THE FUTURE FOR THE BOAT Club? Not surprisingly the club's fortunes have ebbed and flowed over the years. Records have constantly made reference to membership, the difficulty of collecting the subscription - even to a Garda raid on non-members drinking in the bar after hours. Rules are amended. Personnel change. Committees come in and go out. Trustees remain with ultimate responsibility. The subscription which was still at £11 in 1970, went to £17, to £55 and on up as the economic situation changed. By 2004, apart from the joining fee, it was €290 for an adult and €470 for a family - still great value for club facilities in a delightful setting.

It becomes harder and harder to keep Wexford Harbour open as the silting up continues and the club co-operates with efforts to keep the marking of the channels up to date. Yet the Slaney keeps on flowing, and more and more young people discover the delights of the river and the fun of playing tennis in the lovely setting beside the estuary. In summer, sails are dotted across the harbour and families picnic at the Raven Point.

In winter and summer the sound of tennis balls can be heard behind the flurry of junior sailors hoisting their sails. The Club Newsletter introduced in 1991 proved an attractive and valuable publication for keeping Members informed about events for the boating and tennis fraternities, while including items of history, current affairs and interesting photographs. The comprehensive club brochure was another welcome addition - a reminder of how things have changed in one hundred and thirty years and just what an amenity this is for Wexford in 2004.

Wexford Harbour Boat and Tennis Club

REDMOND ROAD, WEXFORD, IRELAND.
TEL: 053 22039
Fax: 053 47504
email: whbtc@indigo.ie
internet: http://indigo.ie/~whbtc

ACKNOWLEDGEMENTS

Detail has come from newspapers, Minute books and other writers. However, statistics and local history would be dull without anecdotes. Many people have helped me by answering my questions and providing information through their recollections, photographs and newspaper cuttings. There has been much laughter. I am grateful to them all, and would have made little headway without the treasures from Michael Donohoe and Irene Elgee. In particular I acknowledge the assistance of the following:

Tom Anderson
Ollie Bent
Tom Bolger
Kirk Brady
George Bridges
Harry Cadogan
Mary & Dermot Carberry
Sinéad Casey
Arty Corbett
Coulter family
Betty Cunningham
Barty Curtis
Canon S. deVal
Donohoe family
Mary Doyle
Larry Duggan
Ann & Tommy Duggan
Irene Elgee
Conor Fallon
Eddie Ferguson
Nicky Furlong
Neville Greated
Jackie Handcock
Avril & Robert Harvey
Paddy Hatton
Jack Higginbotham

George Jenkins
Jan Jenkins
Michael Johnston
Joyce family
Geraldine Kelly
Jane Kelly
David Killeen
Róisín Leahy
Kevin Lewis
Dairine Lowney
Joe Lowney
Jim Maguire
Ollie Mahon
Osnat Manning
Sister Agnes & Kevin McCormack
Des McGrath
Kieran McGuinness
Jimmy Meyler
Evelyne Miller
Richard Miller
Callista & Eoin Murphy
Hilary Murphy
Mary Corcoran O'Brien
Sylvester O'Brien
Sylvia and Jimmy O'Connor
Una & the late Pat O'Connor

Jack O'Leary
Bridget & Tony O'Neill
Mary O'Rourke
Jim Parle
Austin Pender
The late Felicity Poole
Declan Power
Hazel Graham Rowe
David Rowe & Chris Wilson
Scallan family
Séamus Seery
Ernie Shepherd
Sherwood family
James Sinnott
Paul Smyth
Ger Tighe
Des Tyrell
T. A. Walsh
Ward family
Chris & James White
Tom Williams

Wexford County Library and
The National Library

Wexford Harbour Boat and
Tennis Club